Praise About the Author

"Mike Huether has written a valuable primer on how to be a successful public servant. He learned these important lessons as mayor of a small, booming city, where the mayor was never out of reach. Voters and candidates alike should use this as a primer on citizenship."

Tom Brokaw

"My first conversation with Mike Huether about his aspirations for public service occurred twenty years ago at one of the most scenic places in South Dakota—Sylvan Lake in the Black Hills. His passion was undeniable.
Less than a decade later, he was elected mayor of the state's largest city and engineered one of the most prolific periods in Sioux Falls history. Mike Huether has a passion and work ethic to serve and lead that is contagious. He writes compellingly on the joy of public service that both he and I have experienced. In sharing his lessons learned, Mike provides valuable insights that I hope will inspire others to find ways to give back, too."

Tom Daschle
Former United States Senate Majority Leader

"In 'Serve. Lead. Win.,' Mayor Mike's style makes the account of his growing-up, his college and corporate experiences, his passion *for service and approach to governance, and his motivation to lead with purpose to make a difference an effortless and enjoyable read. He shares his fast-paced determined style of working with activists, citizen groups, the city council, and civic and business leaders to achieve major successes during his two mayoral terms that advanced Sioux Falls to new heights . . . Essential for current and aspiring elected officials and civic and business leaders."*

David L. Chicoine, Ph.D.
Professor Emeritus/President Emeritus
South Dakota State University

*"Mike's transition from the private to the public sector was shocking, in a good way. Not only did he bring business acumen into local government, he brought excitement! His saying "Get sh*t done" was as contagious as his personality and something the public sector needs more of. My relationship with then Mayor Huether was an important step in forging a working relationship between our respective cities. Whether a friend, colleague or mentor, Mike values relationships, and he knows relationships are essential to serving others. If you want to build your leadership potential and you have a servant's heart, this book was written for you."*

Steve Allender
Mayor of Rapid City, South Dakota

"Mike Huether's mayoral duties were not just to the city of Sioux Falls. During his terms in office, he was also unanimously elected and continues to serve as the Mayor of "PBRville." He earned the honorary title after many years of visionary leadership that helped our event in Sioux Falls become one of the most successful events of

the tour. Mayor Mike not only helped us hit the ground running, he continued to creatively push the partnership between PBR and the community until the event in Sioux Falls became the first in our history to add a day of competition after it had gone on sale. Beyond the mutually beneficial business success, Mike made every person associated with the PBR feel like a welcomed member of the Sioux Falls community, an incredible and uniquely American city that we love to visit each year. So while PBRville may be a fictional place, Mayor Mike has a very real and tangible place in our world as the lifetime mayor of our town, and he was unquestionably the best mayor of any city we've visited in our twenty-six years."

Sean Gleason
Chief Executive Officer, Professional Bull Riders (PBR)

"Mayor Mike, I am glad you have decided to write a book about your journey of public service. As I mentioned to you in a letter while you were mayor, your get-things-done leadership style reminded me a lot of my father's style. At the end of the day, the public is yearning for non-partisan leadership and problem solving. I am looking forward to reading about the lessons you learned and the inspiration for others to participate in public service. We are all in this together. We should all be ready to serve, lead and win."

Russ Janklow
Friend

"A very interesting read, one that will inspire you and get you thinking about your place in life. You can't help but feel the enthusiasm the author has for accomplishing goals. You may find that serving others

is a worthy goal, and as Mike points out, it will encourage you to "leave life better than you found it."

Elmer Karl
President, Karl's TV & Appliance Inc.

"As Mike Huether's former pastor and friend, I am delighted to congratulate Mike on his new book. It is a continued reminder of the very dedicated love and service he had for the people of Sioux Falls for the many years he was their servant as mayor. I am confident that anyone who reads this book will not only be inspired but encouraged to get involved in whatever way possible to help make families, our city, and our country a better place. Thank you, Mike, for taking the time and effort to share your memories and your vision for all of us."

Monsignor James F. Andraschko
Pastor Emeritus of Holy Spirit Parish, Sioux Falls, SD

"Mike Huether had a great vision for a better Sioux Falls and did a great job in building a unified group of business leaders to FINALLY build an event center and indoor pool. Both developments are great successes financially and physically. His true conviction and leadership made these developments assets for many generations. The tennis facility is another testimony to his and his wife's conviction to the city with their personal donation to make this great venue a success. Thanks, Mike, for being our mayor. We are a better city because of you and your family's service."

Pat and Craig Lloyd
Founder LLOYD Companies, Board Members

"In 'Serve. Lead. Win.,' Mike outlines his journey to leave life better than he found it. He was taught this at a young age growing up in Yankton, South Dakota. He illustrates this quest with examples he has found in his personal, business, and public service experiences. His list of elements to getting things done is direct, practical, and insightful."

Koni & Paul Schiller

SERVE.
LEAD.
WIN.

Martin:
Make the most of the days you are given and get things done - Thank you all for caring for and advocating for OUR KIDS. They need you. Great things to come.

10/10/19

SERVE.
LEAD.
WIN.

*Government can
get things done.*

MIKE HUETHER

Copyright © 2019 by Mike Huether

Softcover ISBN: 978-1-949550-16-0
Hardcover ISBN: 978-1-949550-17-7
Ebook ISBN: 978-1-949550-18-4

All rights reserved. No part of this book may be reproduced or transmitted in any form or by any means, electronic or mechanical, including photocopying, recording or by any information storage and retrieval system, without permission in writing from the copyright owner. For information on distribution rights, royalties, derivative works or licensing opportunities on behalf of this content or work, please contact the publisher at the address below.

Printed in the United States of America.

Cover Design: Amy Gehling

Although the author and publisher have made every effort to ensure that the information and advice in this book was correct and accurate at press time, the author and publisher do not assume and hereby disclaim any liability to any party for any loss, damage, or disruption caused from acting upon the information in this book or by errors or omissions, whether such errors or omissions result from negligence, accident, or any other cause.

Throne Publishing Group
2329 N Career Ave #215
Sioux Falls, SD 57107
ThronePG.com

For more information about Mike Huether, speaking engagements, and bulk orders of *Serve. Lead. Win.*, please visit www.mikehuether.com.

Dedication

My Beautiful Bride, Cindy

I have been blessed by many wonderful people in my life. Family, friends, co-workers, mentors, citizens, and countless others have cheered me on and lifted me up as needed. I can't thank them enough.

However, it is my bride, Cindy, that I owe my deepest gratitude. This incredible beauty, both inside and out, has been my best friend, smartest advisor, and strongest ally as I have tackled my life's "magic list", including public service. Folks don't realize the sacrifice a family, especially a spouse, makes when someone they love wants to serve the people.

Cindy is one of God's true stewards and so many people and organizations have been touched by her warmth, work ethic, strength, and spirit. Especially, our family. She has encouraged and supported me during countless, challenging times. She has often said, "Mike, I just want you to be happy."

Honey, I am happy, because the two of us are on this phenomenal journey together. I love you, Cindy.

Table of Contents

Foreword . . . . *xv*

Introduction . . . . *xix*

1. We accomplished so much, and you can too! 1
2. My sixth-grade speech contest 11
3. Corporate America provided the perfect training ground. 23
4. The nest now empty: It's my time to serve 31
5. Nonstop boots on the ground. 37
6. If you want everyone to like you, public service is not for you. 51
7. The time to lead is now: We can't afford not to. 59
8. Take a strong position and don't waiver in the fight 69
9. Find that common ground! 79

10. Working together, there is nothing we can't accomplish 89

11. "Let me tell you how we do things around here" 101

12. "Inch by inch, Mayor, inch by inch" 115

13. Play to win versus playing not to lose 127

14. Don't forget about earned media 139

15. Politicians don't want results, but public servants do 147

Conclusion 157

Government can get things done! 161

About the author 163

Foreword

Mayor Mike sat motionless in the seat of his truck in the parking lot at the University of South Dakota in Vermillion. The battery was dead. No, not the truck's battery; that was fine. The battery of the mayor of the largest city in South Dakota was completely discharged.

Mike Huether had been up before dawn and driven 80 miles from Sioux Falls to his home community of Yankton. The River City's leaders had relentlessly run his pads off all day, seeking and gaining his frank perceptions and candid insights about everything from family-sustaining jobs to community quality of life. After cramming three days of work into a portion of one day, he then drove to Vermillion.

Late that afternoon, behind the parked truck, loomed I. D. Weeks Library. On the second floor were 28 precocious and passionate students eagerly awaiting his arrival. He understood they were well aware of his reputation for challenging, provoking, and inspiring audiences. He knew they had researched, investigated, and probed every nook and cranny of his life. He realized that armed with their ubiquitous smart phones, they would relentlessly fact-check him real-time for three long hours. He was also an SDSU Jackrabbit, venturing into a den of USD Coyotes. Given the draining rigors of his day, the energy to rise to that daunting challenge was missing. He shuffled through the library like a man approaching a firing squad assembled in his honor.

Then, he opened the door to the classroom.

Three tumultuous hours later, the students were exhausted; their batteries drained. Mayor Mike, just getting really revved up, was eager for more intellectual combat, but yet another hour's drive to the north, Cindy—his wife, best friend, and reality check—was waiting with dinner for his arrival. After dinner, perhaps even more adventures would beckon. The day was young, and the mayor perpetually so.

Where does Mike Huether's passion for public service come from? It comes from the people. They challenge and provoke and inspire him. They continually recharge his battery.

In May 2010, when the mayoral candidate the polls proclaimed could not and would not win had won, Sioux Falls was a large town wondering if it dared assume the manifold obligations of a true city. For over two decades, the town had debated if it really could build a truly world-class events center. Since 1962, paralysis by analysis had made an Olympic-quality public indoor aquatic

Foreword

facility seem an impossible dream. For too long, the ticking time bomb of public employee pension plans was the can kicked down the road. The community wondered if it would ever have a premier year-round indoor ice complex and top-flight indoor tennis facilities. Many people had abandoned all hope that the building wherein much of the city's workforce had been serving the citizens since 1933 (when Elvis was born) would ever be replaced by a worker-conducive and citizen-friendly structure. Millions of dollars earmarked for the transformation of the gritty industrial rail yard between historic Phillips Avenue and the town namesake Falls of the Big Sioux River were hopelessly bogged down, and time was rapidly running out.

In 2010, Mike Huether had become the mayor of a community where many of whose residents viewed dramatic changes with self-doubting reactions somewhere between "perhaps we can't" and "maybe we shouldn't even try." Eight years later, when he left office, the community's prevailing personality was "we did" and "we will again." A self-confident Sioux Falls was predicting its future by building it. By 2018, Sioux Falls had grown horizontally, vertically, and emotionally into one of the finest small cities in America. Today, Mayor Huether's influence continues to motivate community leaders across our entire state, testament to the unofficial title people gave to him—the "Mayor of South Dakota."

Mike Huether's *Serve. Lead. Win.*

Mike Huether not only helped fundamentally reshape the city's image and self-image, he also helped transform the office of the mayor of that city. Sioux Falls residents will hereafter expect their mayor to be everywhere—from proposing, promoting, and implementing futuristic big ideas to standing shoulder-to-shoulder with fellow citizens on the front lines when the community battles natural disasters. The people now expect (and deserve) a mayor as proactive and engaged as the entire community the mayor serves.

Sioux Falls is today more culturally, socially, and economically diverse because of Mike Huether. While he was one of many interrelated and reinforcing factors, he also was, time and again, among all the necessary ingredients, the catalyst in the crucible.

This book is Mike Huether's very personal story. It is also the story of how Mayor Mike, his family, his teammates, and also his adversaries together created a legacy and a promise for not just Sioux Falls but for communities all across our state. We are the Great State of South Dakota. We get stuff done.

Marshall Damgaard
McKennan Baby
Graduate Faculty, University of South Dakota

Introduction

I ran my first marathon when I turned forty. I set aggressive goals in everything I do, and that includes the road races in which I compete. My marathon goal was to complete Grandma's Marathon in Duluth, Minnesota, along Lake Superior, in less than four hours.

I remember the day like it was yesterday. It was a cool, overcast day with a slight wind at my back. More than 7,000 runners joined me in the quest. I sprinted to the finish line of the 26.2-mile course, arms stretched high with my index finger pointed to God. I accomplished the marathon in three hours, fifty-eight minutes, and forty-three seconds—one minute, seventeen seconds to spare!

I soon realized that attaining my marathon goal was not the reward. It was the months of training, overcoming injuries and enduring the loneliness, bad weather, and sacrifice of being away from my family. The journey was the ultimate reward.

I served the citizens of Sioux Falls, South Dakota as their mayor from May 17, 2010 through May 15, 2018. Next to being a son, husband, dad, and "Bapa," it was the most rewarding thing I have ever done. Those eight years of public service provided so many incredible memories, some of which I share in this book.

I take the day that God gives me and make the most of it. I work my tail off, share my time, talent and treasure, use common sense and business sense, grow, learn, lead, coach, cheer, love, and pray—always moving forward, taking chances, making mistakes, and sprinting to the end.

I do this in life. I did this in business. This worked well for me in government too.

I am excited for you to read this book. I'm confident that you will find it valuable as you tackle public service and leadership. The lessons relayed come from victories in public service, corporate America, and life, but even more so, from the hard knocks sustained along the way.

Let's get started.

1

We accomplished so much, and you can too!

The lessons in this book will empower you to make great things happen.

Working together, there is nothing we can't accomplish. We proved that in Sioux Falls, South Dakota with an eight-year run of success like no other. We made unimaginable progress in a short amount of time. Heed the advice I provide in the upcoming chapters, and capture similar success for your constituents.

Now, not every victory was attained with overwhelming support from the Sioux Falls City Council. We secured wins in which all eight city councilors supported the measure. Some succeeded when five of the eight voted yes. The most memorable triumphs occurred when there was a four-to-four tie, and I had the honor to cast the deciding vote. In a couple of cases, a mayoral veto was utilized, and because of the unwavering leadership of three city councilors, a very determined mayor, and his administration, it was just enough to move Sioux Falls forward.

Here is a small sample of what Sioux Falls accomplished from 2010–2018.

WE EARNED THE TITLE: "AMERICA'S NEXT BOOMTOWN." Our economy rocked in Sioux Falls, and we enjoyed five straight years (2013–2017) of record-breaking construction. We went from $298 million in 2009 to $739 million in 2017, a near 150-percent increase in only eight years.

We improved wages, benefits, and working conditions, cut our unemployment rate in half, and added thousands and thousands of good jobs. "HELP WANTED" signs promoting blue-, gray-, and white-collar jobs in finance, health care, research, manufacturing, service, retail, and agriculture were everywhere.

For a true boomtown perspective, Sioux Falls grew in population the equivalent size of Aberdeen, South Dakota, the third largest city in the state. Sioux Falls became much more vibrant, and the metropolitan area flourished, too.

WE CREATED A QUALITY OF LIFE SECOND-TO-NONE. We established an environment where graduates, families, professionals, and retirees wanted to stay. Better

We accomplished so much, and you can too!

yet, we developed a community that enticed natives of Sioux Falls and South Dakota who moved away to come back home! Millions and millions of dollars were invested in overdue quality-of-life projects, like a new event center (the 44th busiest for touring events in the United States that operates in the black), a new indoor aquatics facility, new indoor tennis and indoor ice complexes, and refurbished parks, bike trails, and libraries in every part of town. There was, and still is, no better place to live in America.

DOWNTOWN SIOUX FALLS BECAME THE PLACE TO BE. The heart of our city, our downtown, never pumped faster and more strongly. It did not come easy. Public support and substantial private investments provided the catalyst. Controversial decision-making certainly played a role at times. No one now remembers an old parking ramp that was directly over the Big Sioux River in the middle of our downtown. This parking ramp was fully paid for, was consistently full of parked cars and trucks, and served as a cash cow for the city, but I wanted it gone. We destroyed that old, white eyesore! This was only one of many changes that spurred development throughout downtown, creating a beautiful and vibrant place to live, work, and play.

WE REPAIRED, REBUILT, AND REPLACED OUR CITY'S AGING INFRASTRUCTURE. This was our rally cry over the years. We executed it to a tee with more than sixty-five percent of taxpayer funds invested in boring projects like streets and utilities. Almost 500 miles of roads were improved, which is about the same distance as a road trip from Sioux Falls to Gillette, Wyoming. We invested heavily in the infrastructure you can't see, including non-sexy water lines, sewage pipes, and stormwater systems. A sewage line collapse early in my first term became the wake-up call that Sioux Falls and this mayor needed.

OUR FINANCIALS WERE ROCK-SOLID. In Sioux Falls, city government worked collaboratively and provided for our residents, saved for that rainy day, invested wisely, and spent frugally. We built one of the strongest balance sheets and financial statements of any government entity in America. We added money to the general-fund reserves six out of eight years, and secured a 29-percent operating reserve for the city "piggybank."

Our per-capita debt level actually decreased, even with all of the investments executed over the years. It went from $1,751 per citizen in 2010 to $1,728 per citizen in March of 2018. Thanks to city council leaders, fees were increased responsibly, and actual users of services paid a larger share of the taxpayer expenses. What a concept!

WE STOOD TALL AGAINST NEVER-IMAGINED WEATHER-RELATED EMERGENCIES. We conquered

We accomplished so much, and you can too!

one of the greatest weather emergencies in our city's history with the April 9, 2013 ice storm. On top of that, we encountered three one-hundred-year rain events (has a 1-in-100 or 1% chance of occurring in any given year), one 300-year rain event, and even one 1,000-year rain event. Flooding creates a terrible risk to families and businesses, but Sioux Falls reduced that risk substantially because of investments made and partnerships enhanced over the years. In one of my final media interviews as mayor, I was asked what the greatest challenge would be for the incoming mayor. I answered, "It will be the weather."

NINETY-ONE PERCENT OF OUR CITIZENS BELIEVED SIOUX FALLS WAS A GOOD OR GREAT PLACE TO LIVE. Citizen surveys verified our success. The 1,200-plus city employees with whom I was honored to serve were the major reason why. They busted their tails day-in and day-out, and the results showed. This employee team, represented by three organized labor unions, trusted government leadership enough to tackle pension reform. Because they did, Sioux Falls taxpayers will save $300 million over the next thirty years. This was the biggest untold story in my tenure as mayor. I can't wait to tell you about it!

WE RAN GOVERNMENT LIKE A BUSINESS. We brought business acumen into government by educating the employees on its principles and then executing those practices. This impacted processes, attitudes, and results in a dramatic way. Doing it the way it was always done in Sioux Falls city government served no one. This was not easy and not without controversy.

We made expensive investments in technology, training, centralization, facilities, and equipment. Our employees and citizens learned to reach higher, change things up, make a mistake or two, achieve the goal, and then do it all over again—just like small and large businesses cultivate with their teams.

WE SPRINTED TO THE END AND PASSED THE GAVEL WITH A HANDSHAKE, HUG, AND WAVE GOODBYE. If not for term limits, I may have been blessed to lead efforts to capitalize further on the monster wins we captured in the final years of my tenure. We laid a solid foundation with the City Center, a new one-stop business development and customer service building, along with a new music pavilion, the Levitt Shell, that will prove to be the perfect event center for our downtown.

The opportunity to lead the downtown rail-yard-redevelopment effort is the undertaking I miss the most. This is one project during my eight years of public service that almost did not cross the finish line. We got it done "inch by inch." Inking the deal that moved this forward, and the development that will occur because of it, will prove to be the most important accomplishment in our

We accomplished so much, and you can too!

city's history. Future mayors, city councilors, investors, and citizens will dream big and build something grand on these acres that will stand tall for generations.

SIOUX FALLS OVERFLOWED WITH CONFIDENCE. There was nothing we could not overcome or conquer, and we proved it time and time again. Working with hard-working city employees was a pleasure, collaborating with fellow elected public servants was an honor, and serving the citizens of the city I love was a dream come true. And finally,

WE GOT THINGS DONE IN GOVERNMENT. And you can too. Take the real-life lessons I relay in this book and make great things happen for the citizens and the communities you serve. I will be cheering you on, and so will countless others across America. All of us value your stewardship, but we need determined leadership from you even more.

2

My sixth-grade speech contest

The difficult times in your life will lay a solid foundation for the challenges, and ultimate rewards, to come.

I am a Baby Boomer born in 1962 in Yankton, South Dakota. My dad, Mynard, had a very outgoing personality. He sold everything from insurance, cars, and water conditioners to pressure cookers, and late in life worked in flea markets from town to town. My mom, Diane, the rock of the family, worked for thirty-five years as the head nurse at the South Dakota State Hospital, providing care and kindness for those afflicted with mental-health illnesses. I often tell people about my parents by saying, "My dad walks into the room and immediately wants to know everyone's life story. My mom walks into the same room and wants to find out who is hurting in any way, so she can take care of them." I like to believe I inherited their best qualities.

My dad struggled with alcoholism most of his adult life and had a hard time settling down, always searching for the next big thing. When I was ten years old, my dad came home and relayed big news to my mom, my three younger siblings, and me. He purchased the St. Charles Hotel and Café in the small town of Parkston, South Dakota, just a couple of miles north of Tripp, where Mom and Dad grew up. He heightened that surprise by buying a farm two miles north of Parkston, where he believed he could raise hogs and horses, as well. Soon after the revelation, we left my hometown of Yankton, with Mom giving up her career as a head nurse. We began our new journey, and certainly hoped for the best, but our family, except for maybe Dad, knew that challenges were not far ahead.

I have a few fond memories of my short time there, but for a fifth-grade first-born of the family, the need for me to grow up fast was tremendous. For example, Sundays at the café were always busy, with families from all over Hutchinson County coming in after chores or church. Folks would drive for miles for our special pressure-cooked fried chicken and Joe Joe potatoes (cut four ways, breaded, and fried with the chicken). Mom and Dad did whatever was required to keep the doors open. Support

My sixth-grade speech contest

staff was kept to a minimum, so I would actually run the cash register on the busiest of days.

Funds were so tight in the family that we kept the food scraps from the café each day, including the old grease, put it in big buckets, and hauled it to the farm as feed for the pigs. Dad's drinking and our family's challenges only got worse, with Mom bearing the burden of trying to deal with them. After less than a year of living in our new place, I was sitting in class one day when I was called to the principal's office. Mom, Gregg, Vicki, and Vaughn were waiting there. Mom said, "Mike, we are moving back to Yankton." It didn't take long to figure out that Dad was not coming with us.

It was 1972, and the stigma of divorce back then was terrible. Mom was doing everything she could because Dad's support was limited at best, and we were barely scraping by. I had bad buck teeth, a "Helmet Head" for a haircut, and holes in my underwear and socks that our Grandma Polly would patch. Mom sewed red-velvet fringe to the bottom of my jeans so they could be used a couple months longer. We lived on the poor side of Yankton on East 12th Street alongside other families with limited means. Native American families lived in shacks across the street, often with no heat, water, or food. I remember Mom welcoming dirty and hungry Native American toddlers into our home, giving them a bath and something to eat. I worried that their parents would be furious with Mom, but they would just take back their kids, not saying much in return. They were thankful, but proud, too.

Growing up then was very hard. I was sad at times, and yes, often mad. Sorry Mom. Sorry Gregg, Vicki, and Vaughn. I am sorry that my family, teachers, and coaches incurred my anger and unhappiness at the time. Why me? Why my family? What does my future hold? Looking back, even though those times were extremely difficult, they certainly laid the foundation for what I have become.

A turning point in my early years came from a speech contest sponsored by the Modern Woodmen of America Insurance Company. It was during my sixth-grade year at Yankton Middle School, and we were required to speak on leadership, public service, and making a difference. Mom helped craft my speech, and I even used the famous quote by President John F. Kennedy from his inauguration on January 20, 1961. He said, "Ask not what your country can do for you. Ask what you can do for your country." I won that speech contest! It was the boost of confidence that I needed.

Life for our family remained difficult for a long time. I could write chapters and chapters about the trials and tribulations faced by my family. But here is the deal: even

My sixth-grade speech contest

with our struggles, we never gave up on our family, and that included Dad. I am so proud of what my brothers, sister, and Mom have accomplished. And, I miss Dad dearly. I will share more of his story later.

As I got older, I became active in student government. At Yankton High School (YHS), a kid nicknamed "Huey" (now wearing braces to straighten his teeth) followed the old recipes of his dad and mom on how to treat others. I got to know each of my fellow Yankton Buck and Gazelle classmates, their story lines, and I genuinely cared about all of them. I loved the YHS Class of 1980. They appreciated my dedication and elected me as their president our junior year, and then honored me a year later as president of our senior class. The talk of my classmates, teachers, coaches, and others across Yankton was that, "Huey was going to be the governor someday." I believed it, too.

That thought continued when I attended college at South Dakota State University (SDSU) in Brookings, South Dakota. While pursuing a commercial economics degree, I was elected as a student senator in the College of Arts and Science as a freshman and gained an early understanding of the various branches and their unique roles in government. I made an impression, because I was asked to be junior Mara Larson's running mate to become the SDSU Student Association president and vice president, which represents all of the university's students. Mara was hard-working, committed, savvy, and smart, and we were a good match. We were aggressive campaigners, relaying the Mara and Mike platform, and distributing "M and M" campaign buttons with the Peanut M&M logo (no, we did not have approval from Mars, Inc. to do that) all over campus. We won the election convincingly.

Being a BMOC (Big Man on Campus) felt pretty cool, but I soon learned that the power I thought we now had was truly in the hands of the SDSU Administration and the elected leaders at our state capital in Pierre, South Dakota. Governor William (Bill) J. Janklow invited the newly elected student association presidents and vice presidents from all of the state's universities to meet with him in Pierre so he could formally congratulate us and discuss a couple of things. Mara and I drove there in an official SDSU vehicle, and loaded up smiles, confidence, and attitudes full of spit and vinegar. We couldn't wait to relay our plans to the governor. It was our time to be heard.

Governor Janklow, the most powerful elected leader at the time and, arguably I believe, the most dominant and productive elected leader in our state's history, walked into a rambunctious and confident bunch. He offered his congratulations and thanked us for our service. Then,

My sixth-grade speech contest

after a dialogue that he certainly controlled, he relayed, "I have been working with the Board of Regents and the university presidents and we have decided to not allow beer or any alcohol in the dorms." What did he just say? They can't do that, can they? Mara and I were convinced the students would hammer us when we got back to campus.

It was an ice-cold dose of political reality in my early days of public service. Even so, representing my high school and college classmates was a thrill and honor for me. They relied on me to do my best to understand what was important to them and our school. I enjoyed the challenge of taking those wishes and concerns to influential leaders, and then working with them to make things better for all of us. This early public service training hooked me, and I wanted more.

After my sophomore year of college, I returned home to make some money and get a dark summer suntan along the shorelines of the Missouri River. With my high school and college accomplishments, I thought I could get one of those coveted state-park greeter or bank internship roles, but all I would get hired for in Yankton involved washing dishes, cooking pancakes, or laboring through back-breaking landscaping jobs. I had just been elected the Student Association vice president of the largest university in South Dakota. Yet I crawled on my hands and knees in 100-degree heat for minimum wage, grafting fruit trees with immigrants from Mexico.

Even so, that summer in 1982 could not have turned out any better. After a hard day's work in the sunbaked fields of Gurney Seed and Nursery, I ventured out with friends to "Nickel Tap Night" at Hackett's Bar in Yankton. It was then and there that I met a nice, beautiful, brown-eyed girl who also worked for minimum wage as a cashier at the local Sunshine Foods grocery store. That night, Cindy Sue Loecker agreed to go on a date with me.

Before the Saturday night movie, we went to Pizza Hut where she ordered pizza and cheese bread. She listened to my ambitious plans of being in public service and making it big someday. I don't know what did the trick, but we kissed for the first time that night in Vern and Marilyn Loecker's driveway. We continued dating and dreaming for almost four more years. She was the love of my life, so on December 28, 1985, we were pronounced man and wife.

Four years later, on January 19, 1989, my best friend became the best mom to another beautiful, brown-eyed girl named Kylie Elizabeth. Becoming parents changed everything for Cindy and me, and the responsibilities were enormous at first. To make it even tougher, we moved away from our families to Buffalo, New York soon

My sixth-grade speech contest

after Kylie started walking. We had little alternative but to determine this parenting stuff on our own.

One lesson came naturally. The effort invested into Kylie provided innumerable rewards. We both understood how important it was to invest time, love, and energy into our spirited and determined daughter. I never missed a first day of school or trick-or-treat outing until Kylie made it clear that I could no longer tag along. Cheering her on as she captured championships in tennis and dance and sharing that joy with her teammates, their parents, and Kylie's coaches were incredible memories. Navigating Kylie's journey from childhood to adulthood was irreplaceable. But the time with Kylie went by, and continues to go by, way too fast.

She left for the College of St. Benedict/ St. John's University in St. Joseph, Minnesota to pursue a peace studies degree and play collegiate tennis in 2007. Before that time, the three of us would regularly talk at the supper table about serving the people of South Dakota someday. But, the timing of the move was critical. My dad was not around much when I was growing up, and I was not going to do the same thing to Kylie. Waiting for her to leave the Huether family nest before pursuing public service would be the right decision for our family.

My life's experiences built a healthy layer of tough crust on my body for the road ahead. Overcoming the challenges of my childhood, being responsible for family, classmates, and co-workers, falling down, getting back up, enduring painful but necessary life lessons, and valuing tough love was just what I needed. How you respond to the challenging times of your life will lay the foundation for your success, too.

3

Corporate America provided the perfect training ground

Running government more and more like a business should be relished, not feared.

In the early 1980s, jobs were hard to find. The level of unemployment and underemployment across the country was extremely high. In 1982, the national unemployment rate rose above 10 percent. The recession was terrible with skyrocketing oil prices, high interest rates, and low home sales. The Midwest took the hardest hit, as the farm crisis in South Dakota affected big cities and small towns alike. I built a solid resume after graduating from South Dakota State University, as I graduated with honors, served as SDSU Student Association vice president and finance chairman, and had all kinds of summer work experience.

My dream job coming out of SDSU was a paid management-training position with which I could learn corporate America management practices at the highest level. Those roles were rare because of the economic recession of the 1980s, but also because big businesses were hard to find in and around Sioux Falls and South Dakota. However, Citibank had just moved its national credit card operation to Sioux Falls, and it was hiring. I scheduled an interview with Jane Kuper, the employment manager in Citibank's Human Resources Department.

I was an overconfident and brash college graduate with a very specific plan. I told her, "I want to be trained in management by the best within corporate America, and Citibank fits the bill." Jane told me that they had a number of non-management job openings, and she strongly encouraged me to consider them. Again, I reiterated my desire to learn how to be a good manager and business leader from Citibank. I know she appreciated my confidence; however, her reply was direct and simple: "Mike, we don't have a program like that here."

So now what? I was twenty-one years old with a commercial economics degree and college debt to pay off, the economy was poor, and I was unemployed. No matter how qualified or hard working I thought I was, I was going nowhere fast with months of "we don't have that here" job interviews. Then I received a phone call that would change my life, and career, forever. "Mike, this is Jane Kuper from Citibank. You are not going to believe

Corporate America provided the perfect training ground

this, but we are starting a management training program here, and I would encourage you to apply."

There were more than 300 applicants who wanted this once-in-a-lifetime opportunity. Eight ambitious young leaders were eventually chosen for the inaugural Citibank, S.D., NA management training class in October of 1984. We were paid a fortune at $18,000 per year, and for eighteen months we trained in almost all of the departments, learning operations, credit, finance, transaction services, legal, customer service, quality assurance, and more. After finishing the program in 1986, I became a unit manager of the Risk Analysis Unit. I was responsible for a small team of employees, some of whom were twice my age. Citibank gave me a 10-percent promotional raise, which moved my salary to $19,800/year. I now made more money than Cindy, who worked as a medical technologist.

For the next thirteen years at Citicorp, I immersed myself in an incredible but sometimes tough training ground at one of the largest financial institutions in the world. Citicorp is a multinational services corporation headquartered in New York City. Citibank is its consumer division. While a grind at times, Citibank prepared me very well to be a decisive and effective leader. If you succeeded in management at Citicorp, you were ready for anything. We were required to set ambitious goals every year in our budget and operational plans. Then, as we stayed on target to achieve those goals, we would be called back in during the third quarter to reevaluate the old target. The bar was always set higher.

The workdays were long and intense. You didn't want anyone to see you leave for home, even after a grueling day. The intense environment wasn't just in South Dakota. I spent five years in South Dakota, five years in Buffalo, New York, and five years in San Antonio, Texas. I spent a short time evaluating the sales, service, and back-office operations of Citicorp businesses in Europe, too. Achieving ambitious results and doing it repeatedly was the norm, and my personality was made for it. I was the right fit for Citicorp, and Citicorp was the right fit for me.

I had no plans to ever leave the firm, but then Miles Beacom, my first boss at Citibank, became the president of a small but growing privately owned credit card company called PREMIER Bankcard in Sioux Falls. He needed someone to drive its growth and development efforts. I had always wanted to team up with Miles again, and to make it better, this opportunity would get Cindy, Kylie, and me back home to South Dakota. The decision to leave Citicorp, a company that invested so much in me, one I knew so well, and where I achieved so much success, was extremely difficult. I almost stayed, but thanks to the encouragement of my friend Miles, along with PREMIER's owner and head cheerleader, T. Denny

Corporate America provided the perfect training ground

Sanford, I made what turned out to be one heck of a career move.

PREMIER Bankcard was different, especially in size and scope, but because of Miles' Citicorp background and others he recruited from the company, there were similarities, too. Ambitious goals were once again the norm, and we certainly pushed each other to achieve them. We worked incredibly hard, but also created a motivating environment. Employees were made to feel valued, and at PREMIER, fun was part of the work equation. I was the executive vice president in charge of marketing and development and was responsible for growing our company in a profitable, responsible, and compliant fashion. We transformed our product offerings and marketing practices, utilizing direct mail, the internet, television, magazines, and more.

Our efforts paid handsome dividends in growth, compliance, service, productivity, and profit. The PREMIER team built a solid company. We eventually added four more service and collection operation centers across South Dakota, quickly becoming one of the largest employers in the state. In the ten years I was fortunate to be on the team, PREMIER Bankcard grew from a small operation into the tenth largest credit card company in America.

At both Citicorp and PREMIER, I learned the virtues of corporate stewardship. There is, and absolutely should be, more to business than improving margins, increasing shareholder value, and earning profits. I learned to donate time, talent, and treasure, and how to lead causes, organizations, and nonprofits to make a positive difference in the world. Citibank laid the foundation for charitable giving all across South Dakota, and First PREMIER Bank/PREMIER Bankcard took it to the next level. I am incredibly proud to be part of Citi's and PREMIER's legacy of giving back to the communities where their employees and customers live, work, and play.

So many valuable lessons were taught, and rock-solid values instilled, during those formative years in business, laying the groundwork for the public service role that would come soon.

4

The nest now empty: It's my time to serve

Don't let anyone talk you out of pursuing your dream of public service, because we need you now, more than ever.

I had a tough childhood in a family of limited means and respect. I was always determined to change that. After twenty-five years in corporate America, exceeding goals year after year, I accumulated wealth and influence. The money allowed me to purchase anything and travel anywhere. The influence provided me with an appreciated level of respect in school, business, and community. Even so, I felt empty inside, and wanted to find a deeper purpose and meaning. I needed to make a change in my life. It was time to tackle that old sixth-grade public service dream of mine, along with all of the risks that came with it.

Before I go further, I need you to know that my original dream was not to run for mayor. It was to become the governor of South Dakota. My classmates at YHS and SDSU knew it, and so did family and close friends. Over the years, I developed a "Huether For Governor" business plan, contained in a massive binder that laid out my strategy. Chapter by chapter detailed policy, marketing, fundraising, media, volunteers, and more to provide my path to the South Dakota governor's office. The "Huether For Governor" campaign book was regularly being refined by me over the years.

I acquired internet domain names including Huetherforgovernor.com, along with Mymanmike.com. "My Man Mike" has its own story. Late one night, I was on the internet studying websites, policies, and campaign methods of governors in the Midwest. I came across information about Indiana Governor Mitch Daniels and found links to his website Mymanmitch.com. Governor Daniels used the "My Man Mitch" tagline for his campaign in all kinds of ways. I was incredibly intrigued and excited about his approach. I didn't sleep well that night, because my mind raced about the potential of a "My Man Mike" tagline.

The next morning, I went to GoDaddy.com to see if the domain for "My Man Mike" was still available. I entered "mymanmike" into their search field, hit enter,

The nest now empty: It's my time to serve

and then a "working" message appeared. After a short but tense time, the screen popped a message that confirmed Mymanmike.com and others were available. I couldn't believe it. This was so much fun!

Planning to run for governor in South Dakota was easier said than done. I tested the waters by attending functions across the state where party advocates, and those interested in government, gathered. While there, I relayed to anyone who would listen that I had the tools and passion to improve South Dakota. I was not bashful about wanting to serve in an elected capacity someday. I even hosted post-party-function events with hotel-room bathtubs filled with ice-cold beer and coffee tables littered with cheap eats. I hung plastic sky-blue and yellow banners I had designed, with test campaign slogans. It did not take a genius to know Mike Huether would likely throw his hat into the ring someday.

I was not alone in my interest to serve as the next governor. One very popular elected official, United States Representative and fellow Democrat Stephanie Herseth, was rumored to be seeking the office her grandfather once held. My feeling was that if we had a spirited contest in a primary election, neither of us would stand a chance winning as a minority candidate. South Dakota was, and still is, a deeply conservative, Republican-dominated state. The last Democratic governor of South

Dakota was Richard Kneip, and he served when I was in grade school. Representative Herseth kept her decision whether to pursue the role of governor close to her vest.

After months of discussion and advice amongst family and close friends, I made my decision. I decided to pursue the office of Sioux Falls mayor instead. It made sense. The Sioux Falls city charter is written with a "strong mayor" form of government, so the mayor's role is much like a chief executive officer. That matched my corporate America and senior-executive experience. The office is non-partisan, so party politics would have less influence on the campaign and the role. If elected, I could sleep in my own bed at home each night, and Sioux Falls' voters were already familiar with me (or so I thought).

The decision to run for mayor, instead of governor, improved the odds of success. I had big dreams, incredible passion, and boundless energy for a city I loved. However, I could not serve as mayor unless I earned the honor. Let me reiterate that. The harsh reality, then and now, is that no matter your qualifications, passion, and energy, you can't serve the public unless you win.

5

Nonstop boots on the ground

When you campaign the old-fashioned way, you gain a powerful understanding of what the citizens, whom you want to serve, hunger for.

Many thought I was nuts to run for elected public office. The perception of government then, and now, is one of dysfunction. This was opposite of the efficient, quality-driven, service-oriented, production-dynamics business world in which I thrived. Over the years, I told many people about my goal to run for office and they usually responded with encouragement and intrigue. But their reactions were completely different when I actually pulled the trigger. Family, friends, and co-workers asked questions like, "Why in the world would you give up your executive vice president role and career success to pursue something that seems so out-of-touch and kind of crazy at times?"

I had a really good job, a healthy paycheck every two weeks, solid health insurance, and a fulfilling, successful career. I helped PREMIER Bankcard achieve record-breaking results, and it was rewarding to make a difference there. The best part was that I worked with teammates who truly cared for each other. But then, I left the company to try to become the mayor of Sioux Falls, South Dakota.

I immediately faced a harsh reality of leaving corporate America. You can be a devoted, top-notch employee, but when you leave any organization you will be replaced before your chair gets cold. Life and business move on, with or without you, and the sooner you take that to heart, the better off you will be.

I don't remember my last day at PREMIER Bankcard, but I do remember the next. I was so anxious, uncertain, and scared. What did I do? Were Cindy, Kylie, and I going to be OK? Where do I even begin with a mayoral campaign? I know that many avoid difficult decisions in life because of a fear of the unknown, or a fear that those whom they have relied on won't be there for them. Time and time again, my life's challenges prepared me for the tough times that came my way. But this time, I was unemployed, had no place to go, and had few family and friends that believed I could pull this off.

Nonstop boots on the ground

I said goodbye to PREMIER Bankcard in the spring of 2009 and announced my candidacy to be the next mayor of Sioux Falls. I needed help, and solicited gracious volunteers and talented professionals. I was fortunate to work with Hildebrand Strategies in Sioux Falls, a political consulting company with a proven record of success. Steve Hildebrand, the founder and owner of the firm, was an SDSU classmate of mine and someone I confided in about pursuing elected office. Yes, Steve did see the "Huether For Governor" binder.

The "Huether For Mayor" campaign would require more sweat, tears, and time because I would only do it the old-fashioned way. This meant going door to door, business to business, shaking hands, kissing babies, actually listening to, and learning from, the people whom I wanted to serve. The game-plan included having me walk business to business Mondays through Fridays along the busiest streets of Sioux Falls. I started this boots-on-the-ground effort by going to every business, building, and floor in our struggling downtown. The recession was hitting America, and that included Sioux Falls. I heard comments such as, "Mike, we are barely hanging on. We are just trying to figure out how to cover the next payroll." There were struggles all over town, with empty storefronts, closed up buildings, limited job openings, and feelings of despair. Confidence was in short supply.

Mike Huether's *Serve. Lead. Win.*

I went from campaigning in shiny-black dress shoes, to pheasant-hunting boots (suitable for the field), to insulated deer-hunting boots (intended for extreme ice and cold), and finally tennis shoes. I left "Huether For Mayor" brochures in as many employee break-rooms as the front desk receptionists would allow. On the weekends, I campaigned door to door, engaging families in neighborhoods all over town. I parked my old, 2002 Dodge Dakota truck, a.k.a. "The My Man Mike Truck," in the most visible locations possible. The tan four-door pickup was easy to spot, as it was covered in bright sky-blue and yellow vinyl "My Man Mike" logos and our campaign's domain address. Eventually, citizens of Sioux Falls got the impression that "this Huether guy" was everywhere.

Not everyone was thrilled to see me or the "Huether For Mayor" volunteers at their homes, businesses, or community events. Doubt crept in quite often. For example, my volunteers and I campaigned outside the entrance of the local Sioux Empire Fair for a full week of August wind, dust, heat, and funny looks from passersby. *What is this guy doing? Do his volunteers know he has no chance of winning?* During the winter months, I froze my butt off standing alone in front of local high schools during big rivalry games. As Knights, Patriots, Rough Riders, and Warriors basketball and wrestling fans walked into

Nonstop boots on the ground

schools and gymnasiums, I remember their "oh, he looks miserable" expressions.

Regardless, my campaign team and I stayed in the fight. Remember, to accomplish extreme goals, you have to face and overcome the scrutiny of those who doubt you. And, more importantly, you have to snub the voices from within that say "you can't do this."

It was now January 2010, and after campaigning for six months, I wanted a sense of how we were doing. We invested in a poll. As expected, the results showed that most eligible voters in Sioux Falls were still undecided. What my advisory team and I didn't expect was that I was ranked fifth out of six candidates. What was more troublesome was that my name identification percentage was in single digits. Are you kidding me? After all of that time and effort campaigning? Soon after, the "Huether For Mayor" advisory team and I held an important meeting to get on track.

Sitting around the dining room table at our home, I told the team that I did not believe the poll numbers. When you campaign the old-fashioned way, meeting people face-to-face, showing up at businesses, neighborhoods, and events across the community, you get a powerful sense of what folks are thinking. That is better than any paid scientific poll. Because of my "burn up the shoe leather" effort, I sensed the pulse of the citizens of Sioux

Falls and what issues and opportunities were important to them. I was confident that my support among the voters was much stronger than the poll numbers relayed.

I also believed that City Councilor Kermit Staggers was in first or second place. Like me, he campaigned the old-fashioned way, going door to door just like he had always campaigned. Councilor Staggers was a university professor and also a long-time elected official. He served eight years in the South Dakota state legislature, and then served on the Sioux Falls City Council beginning in 2002. Throughout his public service, he earned a strong reputation as a fiscal conservative and almost always strayed from the majority when it came to investing taxpayer dollars. On the city council, he would often provide the sole "no" vote, thus developing a nickname, "Dr. No."

My advisory team questioned my judgment in ranking Councilor Staggers so high as they didn't believe he had that large of a following. However, after engaging so many Sioux Falls citizens, I was fully aware of his appeal, especially among "maintain the status quo" and "limited government" groups. With six candidates running, the votes would be divided enough so his loyal base could carry him to a runoff election.

During the meeting, my advisory team also asked, "What is the one topic people are talking about the most?" It wasn't the economy, jobs, bad roads, or crime.

Nonstop boots on the ground

The hottest topic by far was the event center—more specifically, the need for a new event center for our city, as the old Sioux Falls Arena built in 1962 was well past its prime. Anyone in the area who craved big-time entertainment ventured to Fargo, North Dakota, Minneapolis, Minnesota, Omaha, Nebraska, or Sioux City, Iowa. The biggest shows we landed at the old arena were 1970s and 1980s rock bands.

The annual Shrine Circus and the South Dakota State Basketball tournaments also drew some warm bodies to the arena's old wooden, fold-down chairs. But even when they did, the lines for decrepit bathrooms, especially for women, were so long that ticket-holders missed the good parts of the performances. Limited food and beverage options consisted of hot dogs, nachos, popcorn, dill pickles, and a couple choices of fountain soda or tap beer.

The residents I talked with all across the city wanted somebody to finally get a new event center built for Sioux Falls. I had a unique plan to accomplish this feat, and I felt it made common sense, business sense, and fiscal sense. After deliberating with my advisory team, we decided to focus our final marketing push on the event center opportunity. Our campaign needed to pull out all of the stops to garner the attention and ultimate support of the voters. If the citizens agreed with my plan, and if they elected me as their mayor, I would provide energy on the event center topic never witnessed before.

After I campaigned almost a full year, I felt confident. I was not cocky, but I thought I was in first or second place among the challengers. I discovered I was sorely mistaken. KELOLAND TV, the most watched television station in South Dakota, along with the Argus Leader, the largest newspaper in the state, combined forces and commissioned their own poll that provided insight into the upcoming election. According to their poll, I was in next to last place out of the six candidates. To make it worse, my name recognition was still very poor, with only one in five of those polled recognizing my name. That was a kick in the gut. Then came a rip to my heart.

My wife Cindy had always believed in me, and many called her "a saint" for her never-ending support. After seeing those poll numbers, the reality that we could lose this thing was real. On Good Friday, April 2, 2010, Cindy and I had planned to get up early that day and greet everyone at the Mayor's Prayer Breakfast, a highly anticipated and attended event each year. But, the results of that poll hit us hard. I felt terrible, but I felt even worse for Cindy. I knew she was sad, scared, mad, and burnt out, too. I asked her, "Honey, are we still going to the prayer breakfast in the morning to greet everyone?" I don't remember what she said, but

Nonstop boots on the ground

I do remember her glaring look. It was a "for better or worse" look.

Neither of us slept well that night, and morning came fast. It was cold and dark at 5:45 a.m. outside of the Ramkota Exhibit Hall, and once again, we were all alone. From the beginning of this campaign, Cindy and I made a pact that no other candidate couple was going to outwork us. There were no other mayoral candidates that joined us outside that morning. We gritted our teeth, smiled the best we could, and shook as many hands as possible.

At about 6:30 a.m., about thirty minutes before the prayer celebration, I looked down the now filled Ramkota Hotel parking lot to the south. Coming toward me was City Councilor Vernon Brown and his wife, Tami. The well-known and popular public servant was also running for mayor, and in the KELO/Argus poll, he was the front runner. He walked towards me and shook my hand with an aura of well-deserved confidence. "Good morning Councilor Brown. Hello Tami," I said. "Hello Mike, how is it going?" the councilor replied. He wasn't arrogant or mean-spirited. Both of them seemed very happy, and more importantly, happy as a married couple—much different than the Huethers.

After we greeted the last of the prayer breakfast attendees, I turned to Cindy and asked, "Honey, should we go in?" I was drained, and I knew she was too. "Sure Mike," she replied. There was that "for better or worse" look again. The Mayor's Prayer Breakfast was already underway and the attendees were in very good spirits, as they always are for this special event. As I looked around the massive floor for a place to sit, there were only a couple of seats left. I noticed two empty chairs, at a table in the far back corner, next to the men's bathroom. Cindy and I could not have been farther away from the head table.

One year later, the two of us would be sitting much closer to the head table of the Prayer Breakfast banquet. Because on April 13, 2010, I made the runoff! It felt like we shocked the world. Councilor Kermit Staggers and I, the two "shake the hands and kiss the babies" campaigners, ended up receiving the most votes. We were separated by only forty-nine votes. Councilor Staggers finished the primary with 24.87 percent of the votes, and I finished with 24.71 percent. Because neither of us received a majority, a runoff election would take place two weeks later.

It appeared to most that the runoff election would be a nip-and-tuck battle. Councilor Staggers and I had very little time to gain the support of the voters that originally voted for one of the other four candidates. Our campaign intensified our strategy, message, and work effort. Councilor Staggers certainly was committed, but his base was

Nonstop boots on the ground

tapped out. His message of anti-growth, anti-spend, and anti-change did not resonate at a time when Sioux Falls needed all three elements to get our city humming again.

On Tuesday, April 27, 2010, the voters of Sioux Falls voted for me, the candidate with no prior public service or "political" experience. We triumphed 57 percent to 43 percent! Election night was one of the best of my life. Seeing the joy and excitement of so many, and knowing we could now fulfill the hopes and dreams of Sioux Falls citizens, was absolutely thrilling. The incredible hard work and sacrifice of so many wonderful family members, friends, and volunteers paid off. They were exhausted, and so was I. I gave it my all, sprinted to the end, and had nothing left at the finish line except thanks and prayers.

I was sworn into office by Judge Charles L. Nail Jr., a family friend, at 2:00 p.m. on May 17, 2010, at Carnegie Town Hall. Four city councilors also took an oath that day, and all of them proved to be pivotal in the years to come. Councilor Sue Aguilar began her second term, and Jim Entenman, Michelle Erpenbach, and Rex Rolfing kicked off their first terms. Like me, they were hungry for progress. After sharing handshakes, hugs, and cake, we started what would become a very transformational, and incredibly productive, eight years in the history of Sioux Falls.

6

If you want everyone to like you, public service is not for you

Secure the minimum votes required, absorb the hits from the critics, execute the plan, and move on to the next big thing.

The most influential people in my life have been my toughest coaches, bosses, and mentors. They never accepted less of what I could give, and always challenged me to do more. I often disagreed and butted heads with them. When I was young I thought I knew best. These leaders impacted me in such a positive way. They knew that there was a chance I may not "like them," or the tough love they provided along the way.

    I have developed my own leadership style, incorporating leadership principles I have learned in sports, family, business, government, and life. Some question my fast-paced style and boundless energy. I strive to win (actually, I hate losing more than I like winning). I encourage my teammates to work harder and dig deeper. The best tough love advice I give is as old-fashioned and corny as you will find. You have to work your butt off! You just do. The harder you work, the luckier you get in anything you do.

Why in the world wouldn't you perform at the highest level to make grand things happen for you, your family, team, employer, and constituency? Hard work is absolutely pivotal to earning wins and overcoming challenges. General Colin Powell once said, "You can be anything you want to be. But wanting to be isn't enough. Dreaming about it isn't enough. You've got to study for it, work for it, and fight for it with all of your heart and soul."

I constantly search for people who take on things that most don't have the will or heart to do. When someone pushes you, even beyond your comfort zone, embrace it and learn from it. Trust me. The time to be concerned in your career or life is when the motivation and constructive criticism is directed toward someone other than you. Demanding more of others, encouraging them to work hard, is not easy, because some won't like you for it. When you address controversial topics in government, more critics and naysayers will be added to your "I don't like you" stockpile.

Governor Janklow served South Dakota as governor for four terms (1979–1987, 1995–2003) and was labeled as

If you want everyone to like you, public service is not for you

a brash and uncompromising type of leader. He accumulated packs of detractors and enemies, the harshest coming from some in the media. Regardless, I believe no one has accomplished more for our great state than him. I am honored and flattered when my leadership style is compared to his.

Governor Janklow influenced my life in many ways, including my career at Citicorp. He directed a change in South Dakota's laws regarding interest rates, which influenced Citicorp to relocate its credit card operations to Sioux Falls. His guts, risk-taking, and fortitude dramatically enhanced career opportunities, corporate stewardship practices, and the way South Dakota does business. By the way, South Dakota is consistently ranked as one of the top states in America for business.

Soon after I was elected mayor, my next-door neighbor Terry Baloun shared sage advice that was a catalyst for our results during my eight years of service. Terry is a retired corporate executive of Wells Fargo and a respected community leader in his own right. He actually served as the co-chair of the Event Center Task Force that my predecessor commissioned. I was not in favor of some of that group's recommendations and developed a different plan to get a new event center for Sioux Falls built. My position was contrary to that of my neighbor and good friend, Terry. Doing this caused great turmoil, certainly risking our friendship. But thanks to the guidance of our wives, especially Terry's wife, Sheryl, and some back-porch conversations, we overcame it. His big brotherly care and advice to me was reignited, and he remains an important part of my life today.

As next-door neighbors, we often chat in our front yards. One beautiful South Dakota day, after I had been serving as mayor for only a short time, we were talking about what I wanted to get done for the city. From Terry's perspective, there were several projects that were long overdue in Sioux Falls, including the new event center, of course.

Terry told me, "Mike, I have some advice for you." I was ready. He said, "Now that you are in government, remember one thing. Fifty percent plus one is a win, and 55 percent is a landslide." At first blush, I didn't believe it or at least I didn't comprehend it. He continued, "Yeah, Mike. In government, if you can just get one more than fifty percent of the citizens or city councilors to agree with you, that chalks up as a win. Then, you can move forward to tackle the next big thing." And then he reiterated, "If you can ever get 55 percent to agree with you, now that's a landslide."

Even the most confident leaders may not be comfortable with Terry's suggestion. What was I to think? I was a rookie mayor, fresh out of the blocks, who had just captured 57 percent of the vote. I felt some people

If you want everyone to like you, public service is not for you

probably thought I was an OK guy. But, if only 50 percent agreed with me on something, that meant that 50 percent would be against me. There was no way I could stomach that many potential enemies on the issues, right? I soon confirmed that Terry's advice was spot on!

In government, if you truly want to get things done, quit trying to please everybody. Stop singing "Kumbaya" and cease seeking everyone's blessing before moving on. Get the minimum votes required, take your hits from those that disagree, execute the plan, and move on. You are not going to accomplish anything if you strive for perfection and appeasement. Make only one promise to those you serve: "I guarantee you, there will be times when we will have to agree to disagree."

Many in government waste time and resources, pining for additional support. "Ok, we better hold more meetings" or "we need more buy in" is often the rally cry. They get hung up making sure everyone is happy. You don't need another meeting, another study, or another vote. What you need is fifty percent plus one, and then move on!

I am not saying that good leaders should make decisions in reckless and uncompromising ways. Leaders need to complete due diligence, collaborate, and find common ground, which takes skill, determination, and hard work. No matter the effort, you will still hear:

"That's not what I would have done." Make tough decisions, take your lumps, and move on in family, church, sports, business, and government. Then, enjoy the satisfaction and success that comes with the decisions made.

There is something else to ponder that may sound a bit contrary to the 50-percent-plus-one recommendation. We should also be concerned with weak entities, boards, committees, and organizations that rarely disagree or debate. Many volunteers clamor to be part of a board, council, or committee, but then rarely add anything to the mix. They enjoy the free lunch and listen intently, but when asked, "Does anyone have anything to add?" Silence. Then, that oh-so-critical vote of approval needs to be dutifully recorded for the monthly minutes. "All in favor say aye. Aye! Opposed?" More silence. You can hear crickets.

It is nice to be included, but members should take a risk, offer a suggestion, get uncomfortable, and even vote "no" if it is best. Some may get upset, but they will move on. They forget. As my dad used to say, "Time heals old wounds."

I want to thank my neighbor Terry, Governor Bill Janklow, and all of you who lead boldly, take hits, and affect real change knowing not everyone will agree. You ultimately garner more respect, genuine friends, and support in life because of the tough decisions you make.

7

The time to lead is now: We can't afford not to

Prioritize the critical items on your constituents' "to do" lists and work to cross them off now!

My dad was diagnosed with cancer the day we celebrated Kylie's 13th birthday. Dad and I were sitting on his emergency room bed when he was given terrible news. He had a brain tumor the size of a large walnut. It developed from lung cancer then metastasized to his brain. Dad ultimately quit his drinking, but he never could quit his smoking. As a teenager, he smoked Marlboros, and then cheaper, but no less deadly, cigarettes as he got older.

Ten days after the cancer diagnosis, my dad, some family members, and I were in the doctor's office preparing for the challenges ahead. At one point, the doctor offered encouragement and said, "Mynard, you have at least a year to live. So, go out there, make memories, and enjoy your family as much as you can." Mynard J. Huether, my dad, died the very next day.

I have always lived my life with a sense of urgency, trying to make the most of the days God gives me. But when Dad died, that zest to squeeze as much into each day was taken to a new level. There are no guarantees we will get another day.

The citizens of your city, state, and country have all kinds of items on their "to do" lists. As a public servant, you were elected to cross them off, so what are you waiting for?

The "what are we waiting for" list in Sioux Falls was extensive when I decided to run for mayor in 2009. Our city just could not get them crossed off. For example:

- The old Sioux Falls Arena, built in 1962, was well past its prime, and major concerts and events went elsewhere.
- Sioux Falls gets bone-chilling winters but had no public indoor facility for swimming. This had been discussed since the early 1960s. By the way, indoor tennis and ice facilities were also severely inadequate.
- The last time Sioux Falls invested in a building where city employees could work and citizens could

The time to lead is now: We can't afford not to

be served was way back in 1933. Elvis Presley was born that same year.

- A $40 million federal-government earmark was secured in 2005 by South Dakota Senators Tim Johnson and John Thune and Representative Stephanie Herseth to remove a rail-yard switching station from our downtown. We had access to the funds, but couldn't navigate the bureaucratic hoops and ladders to utilize them.
- Pension reform. Oh, come on now Mike, no one tackles pension reform. The expenses and liabilities of our pension system, especially exorbitant health care costs, created an out-of-control freight train headed toward Sioux Falls. A similar train is heading to your town and state.

All of these were going nowhere fast in Sioux Falls. To be fair, mayoral task forces were established for the old arena issue. But, the will to tackle the indoor pool and the rail yard government earmark had languished. The "we need a better place for public employees to serve citizens" building issue and the "don't ever touch this" pension topic didn't create headlines, and the political risks were too high for elected leaders. Sioux Falls was knee-deep in the "leave it for the next guy," "wait for the next term," "we don't need it that badly," and "let someone else pay for it" syndrome.

The consequences of waiting to tackle tough issues for your city, state, and country are dire. The old "if you are maintaining the status quo then you are falling behind" adage is absolutely true in life, sports, business, and government. The competition is not waiting. They are making changes, taking risks, learning from mistakes, and making necessary investments.

This is an exciting time, with millennials, job seekers, and the companies that hire them, going to where the action is. When I graduated from college in the early 1980s, my fellow graduates and I looked for jobs, found jobs, and then moved to the cities where the jobs were located. It doesn't work that way anymore.

Now, job seekers search for a community that meets their high standards of where they want to live, work and play. Then, and only then, will they move to that selected city. After that, they look for that new job and employer. Don't forget the retirees, a.k.a. the Active Generation, either. They are also much more selective when deciding where to spend their golden years.

Large and small businesses pit cities and states against each other before ever setting up shop or expanding there. If community leaders and government servants lack the energy, will, and urgency for this fight, their

The time to lead is now: We can't afford not to

biggest worry won't be an inability to recruit new citizens, workers, and employers. Rather, it will be losing the residents, workers and employers they already have.

If that doesn't capture your attention, this will: Waiting to lead can impact the pocketbook of the taxpayer in a dramatic way. For example, infrastructure is only getting older and becoming more expensive to repair or replace. Roads, bridges, and buildings are in sorry disrepair. The things we can't easily see below the surface, like sewer pipes, water lines, and utility infrastructure, are even worse.

On Wednesday, August 4, 2010, I was driving back to the office from an appointment when I received a call: "Mayor, you need to get here immediately. We have an emergency!" Public Works Director Mark Cotter was waiting as I sprinted into City Hall. He exclaimed: "Mayor, we've had a major sanitary sewage line collapse up by the prison. If we don't do something, I estimate we could end up with around 25,000 homes with raw sewage in their basements." Are you kidding me? I had only been serving two-and-one-half months, and I never imagined my first big test would involve sewage.

The magnitude of the emergency was enormous. Thanks to the hard work and ingenuity of Sioux Falls city employees, the media, private contractors, county and state partners, and our citizens, we avoided what could have become one of the greatest health catastrophes in Sioux Falls history. More than 1,000 homes were still affected. We also faced scrutiny over tough decisions that were made, such as dumping one-third of our city's raw sewage into the Big Sioux River at one point.

The harsh lesson was that Sioux Falls waited too long to address the aging and expensive infrastructure of our ever-growing city. The warning signs were everywhere with potholed streets, patchwork fixes to parks and bike trails, a reliance on one-hundred-year-old cement sewage pipes and stormwater systems, and more. For a number of years, the winners in Sioux Falls were those that spearheaded the anti-tax, never invest, "over my dead body" brigades that evolved whenever public tax dollars were needed.

This "oh, it can wait" mantra has spread far beyond Sioux Falls. It is across South Dakota, too. Our economic foundation is based on agriculture. We grow and harvest the finest corn, soybeans, alfalfa, and other row crops. We raise the highest quality cattle, hogs, and other livestock throughout the sixty-six counties of the Mt. Rushmore State. However, we face an issue in which some roads and bridges are in dire shape. We struggle to get record-breaking yields to the grain elevators and livestock to the markets and meat-packing plants. Some "oil roads" went from paved, to potholed, to gravel, and then to dirt, and

The time to lead is now: We can't afford not to

bridges are closed or have load limits due to inadequate maintenance.

The greatest concern lies in the towns that rely so heavily on the economic development impact generated from hardworking farmers and ranchers still living in the area. The dilemma facing these communities of how to pay for public works infrastructure compounds as residents age and the tax base shrinks. Residents hold out hope that the "Mayor, we have an emergency" call does not occur in their town during their lifetimes. However, these calls are sure to come.

One thing that does "light the fire" for an elected public servant is a pending term limit. There is an urgency created at the end of an official's tenure. Time limits produce the extra will to tackle issues. Elected officials find more guts because they can't run for office again, so they don't worry as much about losing votes by taking tough stands. Term limits should be the rule versus the exception in public service, especially in Washington, D.C. New leaders and their innovative ideas should be welcome, versus the establishment's fight to the bitter end to maintain their power and control. American citizens are the only ones who can affect this necessary change, as Congress will never advance this on its own.

South Dakota Governor Dennis Daugaard served two terms from 2011–2019. Before he was elected, our state had the sad distinction of compensating public-school teachers at the lowest level in the United States. Soon after he was re-elected to a second term, the governor was determined to correct this. The scrutiny, even among his own political party, was intense. But, with the support of educators, civic leaders, public servants, and citizens, he rallied support for legislation that increased South Dakota's teacher pay. We are no longer in last place. There is still plenty of work to do, but this was a crucial win for teachers, students, communities, and South Dakota.

Issues and opportunities become beasts for public servants to hunt and slay. Constituents are hungry, and they are anxious for government leaders to capture the bounty. During my eight years of serving the citizens of Sioux Falls, we had a number of very successful hunts. I am thrilled to share the stories, along with the proven techniques, in the chapters to come.

8

**Take a strong position
and don't waiver in the fight**

The citizens elected you to lead, so take the stand that you believe is best and stay strong "in the arena."

Why does government seem to require that perfect solution before moving on? There is an insatiable need for more due diligence, meetings, time, buy-in, and assurance that it won't fail. We could not afford to wait for guarantees in corporate America. There were times when we clashed in the boardroom, struggling how to reach a goal or solve a problem. However, once the jousting was over, and the decision was made, we moved forward as a team and implemented our plan.

Within a few short weeks of settling into the mayor's office, I met with my campaign co-chair, President Rob Oliver of Augustana College (now Augustana University). Rob is one of the most influential leaders in our city, and he would be a great mayor. Rob's leadership style is also heavily influenced by business experience, as he was a senior executive at Wells Fargo. That particular morning, Rob sat in one of the high-backed blue chairs and I sat on the couch to his right.

After some small talk, it didn't take long for Rob to hammer home some big brotherly advice. This swift kick in the butt went something like this. He said, "All right now, Mayor Mike. You told the people of Sioux Falls that if you were elected, you were going to get a new event center built for them. So now, you need to do it."

Rob then backed up his call for action with sound coaching. He said, "You need to take a position that you think is best for the citizens of Sioux Falls, one that will prove successful in getting it done. People are going to disagree with you on this and that, but you need to make decisions, take your hits, and move on."

We discussed areas of disagreement that were certain to come in the event center debate such as timing, size, cost, funding, location, amenities, and so on. He made the timing decision for me, reiterating the time was now. He reassured me that because of the campaign I just completed, I understood this particular need for the community. He reminded me that I was soundly elected, had the courage to drive this, and was capable to take the flak that was sure to come. His message was loud and clear.

Take a strong position and don't waiver in the fight

Soon after my one-on-one with Rob, I developed my own event center advisory team that included members of the city council, civic leaders, key department heads (always include legal support), a project manager, and myself. I needed a nimble, trustworthy, and unwavering group that would work behind the scenes and think outside of the box. Most importantly, they had to be willing to challenge others on the team, especially me.

The person at the top of the organizational chart is key in driving success. He/she must be someone to believe in who will never shy away from the cause. However, it is still the unshakable team around any leader that proves pivotal to the organization's success.

In late 2010, less than six months after I was elected, my advisory team put together a proposal for a new event center. There was plenty of debate and disagreement among the ten of us as the plan developed, but we all felt good about our end result. The plan details included building a $115-million 12,000-seat multipurpose event center that would be connected to the city's current convention center and arena. The city would bond the expense and pay off those bonds with sales tax revenues.

We presented our plan to the public, and the response seemed positive among the city council, media, and the citizens. At a minimum, I followed through with what I said I would do if I was elected.

In the months to come, we answered a barrage of questions and explained the rationale behind each plan component. With multiple elements within our proposal, we had no doubt there would be points of disagreement among the city council and public. We calmed most critics, and stayed on track with the Sioux Falls city council members. This was very important. Even though I was the mayor in a "strong mayor" form of government, the city council had the power to approve the bonds, along with the mechanism to pay them off.

A defining gut-check in the debate concerned one particular component of our plan. Surprisingly, it was not about taxes, finances, or money. It was about "location, location, location." A passionate, organized, and committed group of business leaders and citizens wanted the new event center to be located in downtown Sioux Falls. They believed placing a new event center there would dramatically spur on other development. Also, there were bars, restaurants, and other amenities already downtown that patrons of a new event center would frequent.

Steve Hildebrand, who owned Hildebrand Strategies, the company that managed the "Huether For Mayor" campaign, was their leader. The group could not have found a more seasoned, well-trained, and determined person to drive the "Build It Downtown" movement. Its

Take a strong position and don't waiver in the fight

arguments were reasonable, and the group did a solid job justifying its position.

The site that my advisory team recommended for the new event center was where the Sioux Falls Convention Center and Sioux Falls Arena were located. The Convention Center/Arena site provided plenty of contiguous flat-floor space necessary for large conventions, conferences, tournaments, and other public events. Taxpayers would reap the benefits of existing infrastructure that provided easy traffic access points in and out, ample parking, and utilities. We touted that the Convention Center/Arena site was locked, loaded, and ready to go.

Both sides stood firm and defended their positions. I received a good share of hits, criticism, and second-guessing. There was pressure to hold more meetings, create another mayoral task force, and some wanted me to start over from scratch. Enough already! It was time to put our recommended proposal to the test. We placed it in the hands of the city councilors.

The city council squared off with the "location, location, location" dilemma on June 13, 2011. After hours of public input on this hotly contested topic, the city council was prepared to vote. My team felt confident that we had secured the necessary support for the Convention Center/Arena site location, but pressure-packed settings create "heat of the moment" emotions, so you never know how an elected public servant will react.

The city council first voted on a resolution sponsored by City Councilors Vernon Brown and Greg Jamison. The resolution was to place the event center, if approved, in the downtown Sioux Falls area. Of course, I was hoping the city councilors would vote "no."

I read the names of the city councilors out loud one by one. As each called out their vote, I scratched a line up and down under my scribbled words "yes" and "no." One tally mark under "yes." A tally mark under "no." And so on. The tension was unreal for me, because so much was riding on the outcome. There was no doubt that this vote would determine the future location of the Sioux Falls event center if it were constructed. But it would also be a real test of my ability to lead an important community cause, such as this.

Four of the city councilors voted "yes" to build it downtown, including one city councilor that was a member of my event center advisory team. Four of the city councilors, Kenny Anderson Jr., Jim Entenman, Dean Karsky, and Rex Rolfing, felt the Convention Center/Arena site was a more suitable location and voted "no". It was a four-to-four tie. I wasted no time and said, "the mayor votes no. The motion fails four votes to five." The room was noisy at first, but everyone in the audience remained professional

Take a strong position and don't waiver in the fight

and respectful. The process was difficult, but it was a good one. It was now 11:00 p.m., four hours after the city council meeting started, and we took a short recess.

The meeting, along with more public testimony about the proposed event center location, resumed at 11:06 p.m. As midnight approached, a resolution of the city council supporting the Sioux Falls Convention Center location as the site of a future event center was sponsored by City Councilors Jim Entenmann and Dean Karsky. This time I was hoping to hear them say "yes." Once again, I ended up scratching four lines under the word "yes" and four lines under the word "no." It was now after midnight, my heart was racing, and I immediately said, "the mayor votes yes. The motion passes five votes to four." Pounding the gavel to end the city council meeting that night never felt so good!

Many more and no-less-intense city council meetings would occur in the months to come as additional elements of our plan were scrutinized. After considerable due diligence, the city councilors put the fate of a new event center in the hands of the voters. On August 8, 2011, they passed an ordinance (seven-to-one, Councilor Brown voted no) to call a special election. The proposition to build a new event center stated, "Whether the city of Sioux Falls should build a multi-purposed event center and associated site improvements (the project) at a project cost not to exceed one-hundred-fifteen million dollars ($115,000,000)."

"Build It Now," a committee of community leaders and stewards, including some who initially were not in favor of me as their mayor, worked extremely hard to extol the virtues of voting yes for a new event center. The campaign explained the quality of life and economic development impact a new event center would have on Sioux Falls, the surrounding area, and South Dakota. The "Build It Downtown" team stayed determined and never gave up its fight. Both groups should be commended.

On Tuesday, November 8, 2011, Sioux Falls experienced one of the largest voter turnouts in our city's history. The citizens overwhelming VOTED YES for a new event center by a margin of 58 percent to 42 percent! Later that night, City Councilor Jim Entenman and I walked side-by-side on the hockey ice of the old Sioux Falls Arena. We strode towards an excited bunch gathered for an impromptu press conference, with Metallica's "Enter Sandman" blaring from the speakers overhead.

The city of Sioux Falls has had some big days since being founded in 1856. The leaders and residents of this great city have rallied time and time again to create some wonderful memories over its 150 years. This particular day was one to be remembered. "It is a great time to be a citizen of Sioux Falls," I stated with pride.

9

Find that common ground!

Embrace the differences of your peers, collaborate with them, and find that common ground to make the impossible possible.

More and more people are failing to pay attention to the important issues of our time. Government disinterest is rampant. It is extremely difficult to find citizens willing to pursue public service. Another troubling trend in government should concern us even more. The "my way or the highway" forces are driving a wedge between those who want real progress. They build fortresses around their extremist ideas and strongly oppose anyone with differing views. Getting what they want, and only what they want, is their mantra.

Nothing constructive comes from these all-or-nothing forces. Sadly, the more "in your face" these people become, the more news coverage and social media exposure they receive. This is dangerous, because we are becoming numb to these radical voices along with the measures they proclaim. These loud and media-hungry, divisive entities waste valuable resources and time. Public servants are tempted to knuckle down to their nonstop demands and misinformation versus doing the important work of the people they serve.

We don't tolerate this type of behavior in our homes, so why do we turn a blind eye to it in government? I was taught that if one kid disrupted the family outing, you pulled him/her aside, told him/her to shape up, or they did not participate in the fun. How many of you bite your tongue and grit your teeth when the parent does nothing with an over-demanding child? It ruins the night out for everyone. Government leaders often focus on the tantrums of the loudest, most demanding voices they hear. Listening to them and valuing their passion is one thing, but becoming beholden to them is another.

As mayor, I found great value discovering the common ground. Remember my event center advisory team? I don't recall any temper tantrums, but there were disagreements among us as we hashed out our proposal. We massaged each element of the plan, vehemently disagreeing at times and easily moving on with others. We found common ground and developed a proposal to build a

Find that common ground!

new event center that the city council and the public ultimately supported.

My success as mayor, and the achievements of Sioux Falls, should be credited to team decision-making. The city council, our legislative branch, was imperative to our success. I encouraged councilor participation on my advisory teams, and hosted meetings in my office to garner their opinions and support. This was a challenge at times, because the rules only allowed three of the eight city councilors to meet with me. Any more than three constituted a quorum and needed to be publicly noticed. The extra effort was worth it, because the ultimate buy-in of the legislative branch is crucial to getting things done in any government entity.

The following real-life example of finding common ground should be a case study for every city, county, state, and business in America. Pension reform, or the lack thereof, is one of the most consequential challenges facing business and government today. Yet, the most popular approach to address it is to stick our heads in the sand and leave the problem for the next person. The chief executive officer, mayor, or governor, along with the business and government employees they lead, hope and pray the pension freight train won't derail while they are on the ride.

The original rationale for pensions that the employee works hard, and the employer garners success, remains.

The employer and the employee set money aside, so when the employee retires, a nest egg provides financial security for the latter years of life. This concept is acceptable, but is not as feasible as it once was. In government sectors, exorbitant health care costs and the inability of elected officials to restrain unaffordable demands, intensify this crisis.

When I entered office, the Sioux Falls city government pension system was stable and the benefit plans were well-funded. However, when the pension numbers were crunched for the out years, the expenses and liabilities—especially rising health care costs—showed dramatic long-term risks. Sioux Falls was fine, but it would not take long for this to implode, just like what was happening in business and government sectors across America. I knew it, our human resources and finance teams knew it, and the city council knew it. Reluctantly at first, the city employees also acknowledged the harsh realities of the situation. We had an obligation to address this, because if we didn't, the risks to the city, our hardworking employees, and taxpayers were huge.

The first step was to secure a level of trust from key players such as the Employees Retirement System and the Firefighters Pension Fund Board of Trustees. We completed a comprehensive review of the city's current pension system, including actuarial studies by a

Find that common ground!

third-party consulting firm. The long-term sustainability of the city employees' pension benefit was paramount. We needed to make changes to the pension plan and address the issue with a sense of urgency.

After numerous meetings, the pension boards, the city council, and employee leaders heard the alarm bells and responded accordingly. To their credit, they understood they could be part of the solution now or be a victim of someone else's decisions later. Getting the Sioux Falls city employees to give their go-ahead would be the deal-maker or the deal-breaker. According to South Dakota state law, any changes to the pension system required an affirmative vote of union membership. The odds of success were not good. When something affects a worker's hard-earned pension benefits, any change would be put under a microscope.

But the pieces came together. After I first encouraged our human resources, legal, and finance departments, along with some key city councilors, to tackle pension reform, I did not contribute much other than cheering everybody on. The credit belonged to the pension boards and key members of the Human Resources Department, especially Compensation and Benefits Manager Angie Uthe. Communication was indispensable, along with cultivating a shared purpose and overriding goal to address this concern now. Angie and pension board leaders held more than forty face-to-face meetings, reaching more than 800 of the 1,200 city employees represented by three labor unions.

There was disagreement, tension, distrust, and doubt at times, but ultimately a sensible plan was built. The employees would contribute a greater share to the pension plan, and the City would provide the retirees a flat-dollar stipend to purchase health insurance or whatever they wanted. The city would get out of the health insurance business, and pension plans would be managed and administered by the South Dakota State Retirement System, versus the city doing it on its own.

After almost two years of planning, communication, building trust, and finding common ground, it was time for Sioux Falls city employees to decide. At the end, the parties trusted the process and each other. The city employees overwhelmingly supported the plan with 89 percent of them voting for pension reform! They supported something that few around the United States even begin to evaluate. The team's work and sacrifice will provide dividends for Sioux Falls City employees and Sioux Falls taxpayers for generations to come. Sioux Falls taxpayers will save $311 MILLION over the next thirty years, and our employees have a pension system they can rely on.

Find that common ground!

At a press conference following the vote, I offered the following: "Hey America, this is a great example of how we get things done in Sioux Falls, with no threats, no picketing, and no punches thrown. Instead, we use good old-fashioned common sense, conversation, and compromise."

As a public servant, you are thrown into the ring with others who possess backgrounds, goals, personalities, styles, and strengths dramatically different than yours. Embracing these differences, collaborating, and ultimately finding that common ground will make the impossible, like pension reform, possible.

10

Working together, there is nothing we can't accomplish

Public and private partnerships add strength, vitality, and confidence to the "get stuff done" mix.

As you now know, my first and last boss in corporate America was Miles Beacom. As the leader of the PREMIER Bankcard team, he often encourages them with this simple but effective message: "We will give you the tools to be successful. If you are successful, then PREMIER will be successful. But if our community is not successful, then we as individuals, and we as an organization, will not be successful."

That same philosophy can be applied to the things we do in life, including government service. We are all aware of the dysfunction of the federal government. The United States Congress has extremely low approval ratings, and the biggest culprit is the polarized and partisan environment in which our senators and representatives work. Washington, D.C. may be broken, but in Sioux Falls and South Dakota, working together drives our success.

You can't go on a run of success like Sioux Falls did without collaboration. People all across America noticed. The CNN Network interviewed me and others in Sioux Falls because the network wanted to market our success, hoping to inspire other cities across our great country. Mayors from Houston, Denver, Nashville, and New York City were also interviewed for the CNN series. At one point in the nationally televised program, CNN journalist and host Fareed Zakaria told the viewers that Sioux Falls and South Dakota are "able to do at a state and local level what Washington is failing to do."

Our "secret sauce" incorporates a blend of many ingredients, but the Sioux Falls business community is the spice that makes it special. Government can't do it alone any more, with satisfaction and trust in government, especially at the federal level, at an all-time low. Public and private partnerships add strength, viability, and confidence to the "getting stuff done" mix.

Having taxpayers bear the cost for everything, especially expensive quality-of-life investments, is a thing of the past with naming rights and sponsorship deals of public facilities becoming more common. Investing taxpayer dollars to support privately owned and managed venues is also more fashionable. In Sioux Falls, city taxpayers

Working together, there is nothing we can't accomplish

paid 20 percent of the expenses of long overdue quality-of-life investments, including a three-sheet indoor ice complex built in 2014. South Dakota hockey players actually held their state tournaments in Iowa until the Scheels Ice Plex was opened. City taxpayers contributed a similar percentage to Huether Family Match Pointe, a six-court indoor tennis center, which opened in 2014 as well.

Is the business community in your city or state leading the charge or protecting their turf when it comes to economic development and job creation efforts? In Sioux Falls, businesses compete at the highest level when it comes to generating market share, maximizing profits, and recruiting top-notch employees. At the same time, when it comes to making our city a better place to live, work, and play, the business community collaborates in a big way. The Sioux Falls Development Foundation, the Sioux Falls Chamber of Commerce, Downtown Sioux Falls, and the Sioux Empire United Way are powerful examples of businesses and nonprofits that make Sioux Falls better. A substantial challenge for Sioux Falls and South Dakota is workforce training, development, and recruitment. It will be the private sector's experience and innovation that discovers the solution.

Another private sector entity, the media, plays a critical collaborative role, too. The media's ability to communicate messages that citizens trust via television, radio, and the newspaper (local news still has a good reputation here) is a proven difference-maker as to whether an initiative wins or loses at the ballot box.

Collaboration among government sectors in South Dakota comes naturally, as there is no place for city, county, state, and federal government leaders to hide on these fertile plains. We attend the same basketball games, law-enforcement wild-game feeds, prayer breakfasts, funeral services, potlucks, county fairs, and wherever Midwesterners gather. South Dakota has been built on a premise of neighbor helping neighbor. In the old days, when a barn burned down, everyone in the area pitched in to rebuild it. We rely on that premise, and on each other, still today. The commissioners and mayors of Minnehaha and Lincoln Counties, the governor, South Dakota state legislators, our two United States senators, and our sole United States representative are all a simple but effective 605-area code phone call away.

South Dakota is known as a land of infinite variety. We have differences among us like big city/small town, East River/West River, rural/urban, and farmers/city slickers. Some try to perpetrate a Sioux Falls-versus-the-rest-of-South-Dakota rivalry. I do what I can to minimize any separation and often broadcast: "When Sioux Falls is successful, South Dakota will be successful. When South

Working together, there is nothing we can't accomplish

Dakota is successful, Sioux Falls reaps the rewards as well." Sound familiar, Miles?

When Sioux Falls needed assistance during my eight years as mayor, South Dakota state government leadership was there. They pitched in during unexpected public health and safety emergencies, infrastructure investments in roadways and bridges, job recruitment and workforce training efforts, economic development drives, and more. Due to the alliance of the Governor's Office of Economic Development, Forward Sioux Falls, the Sioux Falls Development Foundation, and the City of Sioux Falls, the largest commercial development park in South Dakota became a reality in 2015. Foundation Park, an 800-plus acre mega-site located at the intersection of Interstates I-90 and I-29, gives Sioux Falls and South Dakota a distinct advantage when competing for large-scale commercial investments. You need to check us out!

One example of working together in Sioux Falls will always be remembered. It began April 9, 2013. I woke up at 5:25 a.m., brewed a strong cup of coffee, and went outside to get the newspaper. There was a light mist and just enough cold in the air to create a thin layer of ice. I walked with caution. Cold temperatures and light rain are rarely a problem for any winter-hearty South Dakotan, but this situation would prove different.

Mike Huether's *Serve. Lead. Win.*

I drove to work in my Nissan Titan around 7:30 a.m. and noticed the roads were slick but manageable. The temperature gauge on the dash showed 32 degrees, and the moisture was coming down at a heavier clip. Layers of ice were developing on roads, trees, power lines, sidewalks, homes, and businesses across our city.

After glancing out the windows of the mayor's office later that morning, I pulled up a local television weather report on the internet. The Sioux Falls temperature still hovered around 32 degrees, and the Doppler Radar showed ominous colors on the screen, meaning additional precipitation was on the horizon. This "blob" was not going away any time soon.

In the hours to come, tree limbs crashed to the ground, roads became treacherous, power outages occurred, and Metro 911 was inundated with emergency calls for help. Concerns grew by the minute. We were hammered with a lethal combination of rain, ice, heavy snow, strong winds, and thunder. Yes, I said thunder!

An effective government is made for situations like this. We mobilized our Emergency Operations Center to coordinate the massive effort required for the emergency situation. Sioux Falls, a city of seventy-five square miles, with 3,000 miles of roads, seventy-five parks full of trees, 170,000 residents, and countless workers and

Working together, there is nothing we can't accomplish

guests from out of town, was looking more and more like a hurricane zone.

The next morning, we held a press conference to reassure our citizens that we would prevail. Building confidence would prove tricky, because ten more inches of snow were predicted for that night to exacerbate the emergency conditions. I said: "We will get through this, Sioux Falls. However, everyone needs to realize our recovery won't take days or weeks. This is an unprecedented event for all of us, so this will take months. With tonight's forecasted six to ten inches of snow, it is going to get more challenging. Our immediate goals include restoring power, keeping our citizens safe, and clearing the roads of debris so we can plow the snow again tonight and tomorrow. We have until 7 p.m. tonight before this monster storm hits us with another blow."

I continued, "We have declared a State of Emergency in Sioux Falls so that we can utilize all available resources, public and private, to tackle the immediate and long-term challenges associated with this storm. Our city is very strong financially, so we can hire private contractors to assist us in tackling this massive effort to clear debris on every street, block, business, and home in our city. Effective government does this for its people. Safety remains our number one priority, and I am so pleased

Sioux Falls has had only one weather-related injury to date. The men and women of your city, county, and state governments are truly going the extra mile. I am incredibly proud of them, just like I am of all of you! We have a long way to go before this is over, so remain positive, stay patient, and most importantly, keep you and your families safe."

I could, and maybe should, write another book about how we overcame the now infamous "April Ice Storm." The word "team" exemplifies how Sioux Falls conquered one of the most challenging weather-related emergencies in our city's history. For twenty-one days, our Emergency Operations Center remained in place, prioritizing objectives, executing incident action plans, and coordinating the courageous efforts of city, county, state, and private contractors. Sioux Falls was one of the most vibrant and beautiful cities in America before the storm, and it became more vibrant and beautiful when it was over.

It was a grueling battle. We executed an eight-month recovery effort called "Operation Timber Strike." By the end of the operation, city and contracted crews ground and hauled away 55,000 tons of debris, removed 25,758 hazardous hanging branches, 972 hazardous trees, and 1,383 stumps. The cost of the response and recovery operations reached nearly $8 million with the Federal

Working together, there is nothing we can't accomplish

Emergency Management Agency (FEMA) and the United States' taxpayers reimbursing Sioux Falls for nearly $6 million. When FEMA came to survey our progress, Ron Pevan, FEMA Region VIII Public Assistance Coordinator, was amazed. He said, "Sioux Falls conducted the absolute best debris operation from start to finish I have ever been involved with."

It never ceases to amaze me or other Americans how we always work as a cohesive team during times of crisis and tragedy. We rallied as one after the attack on Pearl Harbor on December 7, 1941, and after the tragic day of September 11, 2001. In South Dakota, we cared for our neighbors, just like our ancestors taught us, after the devastating Rapid City flood on June 9, 1972, and the ferocious tornado in Spencer on May 30, 1998. And on April 9, 2013 and the months after in Sioux Falls, South Dakota, we proved that government works incredibly well when its leaders, public and private, work together. There is nothing that can't be accomplished when we do!

11

"Let me tell you how we do things around here"

Listen and learn from special interests, but do not become beholden to them.

I am inspired by strong leaders who exude passion and fight for causes. I eagerly cheer for people and organizations that make a positive difference. However, when I campaigned for and served as mayor, I made one thing very clear: I would listen and learn from passionate leaders of special interest groups and causes, but I would never become beholden to them. I have worked with politicians who believed their best path in public service was to rack up special-interest votes and campaign dollars. I detest this approach, and have no respect for politicians that give it chase.

The word "beholden" was first used in the 14th century. The Cambridge English Dictionary defines it as: "feeling you have a duty to someone because they have done something for you." A "special interest group" is defined as "a group of people who have particular demands, and who try to influence political decisions involving them."

Soon after I was elected mayor, a prominent Sioux Falls developer came to my office to discuss the economic challenges at the time, goals for his company, and how city government can and had bolstered their efforts. At one critical juncture in our conversation he told me, "Mayor, now let me tell you how we do things around here."

After letting his comments sink in, I responded in a direct but well-intentioned fashion. I said, "Well, that may have been the way it has been done around here, but that won't be the case now that I am serving as mayor. I value and respect what you, your business, and the development community do, and I look forward to working with all of you. But any decision I make as your mayor will be based on what I think is best for this city and our citizens as a whole." His tone and demeanor hardened, however he remained professional. After more small talk, we shook hands and he departed. I have little doubt that word of our conversation spread quickly.

What I value most about this particular interaction, is how the two of us, along with our teams, worked so well together over the years that followed. They shot

"Let me tell you how we do things around here"

straight with me, and I did the same with them. We enjoyed standing side-by-side at ribbon cutting ceremonies for their rental housing, retail, and commercial developments during a time when their company, and our city, flourished. I miss working with them.

All of us have causes that excite us. The more we invest in them, the stronger our drive to rally behind them. Special-interest causes, and the people that support them, mean well. However, when well-intentioned groups become unwilling to compromise, wanting only what they want, problems start. These forces can affect the thoughts of elected officials and citizens, in some cases placing blame, guilt, or shame upon them. For example, "You must not care about us or our families," or "You are going to kill our property values and livelihoods," are common themes expressed by the NIMBY (Not In My Back Yard) forces.

A public servant can feel threatened, not with a physical attack on person or property, but with verbal assaults and misinformation. This "stuff" is fed to the media, and then the disagreements, anxiety, concern, and chaos is often dispensed to the public. This creates a much greater perception of strength for these special interest groups than they deserve. When you combine the pressure-packed methods of the CAVE (Citizens Against Virtually Everything) forces, many public servants retreat because of the drama. "I have had enough of this," "I am not going to jeopardize my political career over this," or "I have better things to do," become common refrains.

Don't give up. Do what is right versus what seems safe. Recruit others with strong backbones to stand beside you. Meet face-to-face with these groups, and kill them with kindness and professionalism. Make tough decisions, and remember, not everything needs to be placed on the ballot for the voters to decide. The citizens elected you to lead, and that includes casting tough votes on controversial topics. Ignore the "we will remember this when it comes time to vote for you again" threats.

Respond with the facts, as the most rabid forces want nothing to do with the truth. Some will never compromise, because they relish creating dysfunction and conflict. They thrive on the attention, especially the lights and cameras of the media. Don't waste your time with the extremists you encounter. The citizens you represent will see them for what they really are, and they will soon be old news.

This won't surprise you, but it gets cold in South Dakota. Wind, rain, snow, and ice challenge us at times. We are not like Minnesota with 10,000 lakes, but we still enjoy water activities. What will surprise you is that Sioux Falls did not have a public indoor pool before I became the mayor. Smaller cities in South Dakota like Madison,

"Let me tell you how we do things around here"

Brookings, Watertown, and Yankton invested in them, but the state's largest city in the state would not take the plunge.

Sioux Falls' first attempt at constructing a public indoor pool started way back in 1962, the year I was born. Sioux Falls needed another high school back then to serve its growing population, and an indoor pool was included in the initial building plans. The pool portion of the project was eventually scrapped. Forty years later, in 2005, Sioux Falls made another run at it. A mayoral task force recommended designating public funds for a $32.3 million recreation center offering swimming, hockey, soccer, and more. It was to be located at Nelson Park in Sioux Falls, a site commonly known as Drake Springs Pool. To their credit, they got the proposal on the ballot, but the citizens soundly rejected it by a two-to-one margin.

Two years later, another valiant attempt was made with a scaled-back version of the Drake Springs recreation complex. A neighborhood group against the plan worked to get an initiative on the ballot to build an outdoor pool complex at the park instead. Because of the weather, outdoor pools are only useful seventy-five to ninety days a year in this area of the country. That didn't matter. On May 15, 2007, the citizens voted overwhelmingly, 64 percent to 36 percent, to build another outdoor pool complex in Sioux Falls.

I was determined to get the public indoor pool issue hammered out. I was not alone in this desire. A survey of Sioux Falls citizens showed 60 percent agreed a public indoor pool was needed. I was just as committed to tackle long-awaited indoor facilities for tennis and ice sports, too. It made no sense, and was embarrassing, for a community of our size, stature, and financial strength to not have an indoor place for the public to swim, skate, or play tennis.

One month after I was elected, my administration incorporated the necessary language for future indoor facilities for swimming, hockey, and tennis into the city's five-year Capital Improvement Plan. The justification for the indoor pool included: "This facility will potentially provide recreational swimming, swimming lessons, and competitive swimming, including swim meet competitions to the city year-round . . . . The site has not been identified and will depend on land availability and opportunities."

I set a goal to get this quality-of-life investment approved by the end of my first term. I went through my normal checklist on how to get projects completed by creating an advisory team, completing due diligence, hiring consultants, devising a plan, and educating the city council and public. My administration proposed to build an indoor aquatics facility that would include a zero-depth entry pool and a leisure pool with twenty-five-meter lap

"Let me tell you how we do things around here"

lanes, a lazy river, and water slides. The venue would feature a therapy pool, a fifty-meter lap pool with ten lanes, diving boards, seating for 500 spectators, and other amenities such as party rental rooms.

We hired a consultant to determine the most suitable location, just like we did with the event center. One site emerged above all the others. Spellerberg Park in Sioux Falls was selected for a number of reasons including: its centralized location, its ease of access including public transportation, and its more than eighteen acres of land and green space. The park had an existing forty-six-year-old outdoor pool that was past its prime and in need of replacement. Our plan was solid, the time was right, we could afford it, and the recommended location seemed ideal. Oh no, did I say location again?

Some of the neighbors near Spellerberg Park did not want such a grand-scale facility so close to their homes. They organized the "Save Spellerberg Park" group. Their arguments against the new indoor aquatics center at Spellerberg included: it was important to preserve the existing green space and maintain the traditional atmosphere of the park, replacing the existing outdoor pool would cost less than building an indoor pool, the indoor complex would cause parking, traffic, litter, and crime problems, and surrounding home and business values would deteriorate.

Then another contentious point emerged. One of our nation's best Veteran Administration (VA) Hospitals sits adjacent to Spellerberg Park. The hospital cares for thousands of veterans and their families. The "Save Spellerberg Park" contingent said if the indoor aquatic center were to be built, swimmers and guests would park illegally in the VA Medical Center parking lot. This would impede veterans' access to the care they so richly deserved. No one took this argument lightly, because it involved veterans and their families who had already sacrificed plenty.

The indoor pool debate went on for months and became heated at times. I was hoping that the city council would be able to vote on its own to move a new indoor pool forward. Instead, the controversial topic went to the voters once again because a petition was filed. Ultimately Initiated Measure 2 was placed on the April 8, 2014 municipal election ballot.

The "Save Spellerberg Park" group put its stake in the ground, asking voters to decide if they wanted to replace the existing outdoor pool at Spellerberg Park with a new and larger outdoor pool. It would be constructed for no more than $7.5 million and no later than December 15, 2015 as a replacement for the current outdoor swimming pool. The size and scope of the new swimming pool complex, including parking, would not exceed the size of the current complex by 20 percent.

"Let me tell you how we do things around here"

A different group called "Community Swim 365" went a different direction. It organized its own campaign, which promoted our plan recommending the indoor pool complex at Spellerberg Park. After almost sixty years of debate, the citizens of Sioux Falls would decide if they wanted to invest in another outdoor pool or invest in an indoor one.

It would not be the only thing citizens would vote on during that election. They would also determine if they wanted to keep Mike Huether as their mayor and whether to re-elect two city councilors to a second term. Other important elected offices and measures were on the ballot as well.

The voters would vote whether to rezone property on the south part of Sioux Falls to allow a new Super Walmart to be built there. The "Save Your Neighborhood" group gathered enough signatures to put the "Walmart" Referred Measure, Referred Law 4, on the ballot. This was the most intense NIMBY battle I was involved in during my eight years of public service.

The day after the election, the Sioux Falls Argus Leader ran a story titled "Huether Earns Another Term as Mayor." It kicked off with: "Sioux Falls voters backed Mike Huether's high-energy, take-all-comers style on Tuesday, returning him to the Mayor's office for another four years." I earned 56 percent of the vote, while my

Mike Huether's *Serve. Lead. Win.*

challenger, City Councilor Greg Jamison, received 44 percent.

It went on to report: "Huether's influence could be seen down the ballot as incumbents Rex Rolfing and Michelle Erpenbach, largely seen as allies of the Mayor, were returned to the City Council." Both were re-elected overwhelmingly with Councilor Rolfing getting 58 percent and Councilor Erpenbach garnering 60 percent. For four more years, they would remain allies of the citizens as a whole, never backing down or catering to one particular cause or group.

The article added: "Following the trend, a Huether-backed plan for Walmart at 85th and Minnesota Avenue won wide approval from voters, while a plan to replace an outdoor pool at Spellerberg Park, which he did not support, was defeated."

The anti-Walmart or "Save Your Neighborhood" group was unsuccessful by a margin of 36 percent to 64 percent, and the pro-outdoor pool or "Save Spellerberg Park" group lost by a margin of 29 percent to 71 percent.

The new Super Walmart and the new $23.7 million indoor pool, called the "Midco Aquatics Center," have exceeded expectations. There is booming construction and economic development at one location, and winter and summer attendance exceeding forecasts at the other.

"Let me tell you how we do things around here"

Both of these areas have become very favorable places to live, work, and play.

The newspaper article relayed something else: "Huether overcame a focused assault from City Councilor Greg Jamison, who characterized the Mayor as a man who plows through rather than reaching out to the people who disagree with his policies." I respectfully disagree. Just because I didn't always agree with the person, group, or policy, doesn't mean I "plowed through" them. I did my best to listen to them. And, I always learned from them. But I never became beholden to them.

12

"Inch by inch, Mayor, inch by inch"

Overcoming dire situations and extremely difficult projects requires dogged determination among unwavering allies.

South Dakota and Sioux Falls rely heavily on railways to move goods such as grains, ethanol, frozen foods, and minerals. For 150 years, Sioux Falls was fortunate to have a rail-yard switching station. However, having it located in the center of our growing city was no longer fitting. We needed to find the vision, will, and money to relocate the switching yard from downtown. Accomplishing this would improve public safety, traffic congestion, noise pollution, and most importantly, generate economic development opportunities for downtown Sioux Falls.

In 2001, community and government leaders completed the first step with a project feasibility study and

Mike Huether's *Serve. Lead. Win.*

followed that up in 2002 with a concept-phasing plan. It didn't take long to realize that the monstrous project would require an incredible partnership effort. Partners included the rail companies of Burlington Northern Santa Fe (BNSF) and Ellis and Eastern Railroad, the Department of Environment and Natural Resources (DENR), the Environmental Protection Agency (EPA), the Federal Highway Administration, the State of South Dakota Department of Transportation (DOT), hired consultants, and a wide range of elected leaders representing Sioux Falls and South Dakota.

It would also require an enormous amount of money. Thanks to the efforts of South Dakota's Congressional delegation, most notably Senators Tim Johnson and John Thune, a $40 million earmark was secured in 2005 (one of the last federal earmarks Congress ever approved). Securing these dollars was a huge step, but meeting the federal government requirements to timely spend them would prove to be formidable. No one predicted it would take ten more grueling years.

The original 2002 concept-phasing plan called for putting a curved wye bridge (connects three ways and is shaped like a Y) with railroad tracks over the Big Sioux River near our city's namesake park, Falls Park. The federal government had numerous safeguards to protect public parks such as this, so the plan faced immediate environmental challenges and financial burdens. Moving

"Inch by inch, Mayor, inch by inch"

the rail-yard switching station from its downtown location was also extremely complicated. The proposed new location, just outside of town, fueled a bunch of NIMBY squabbles.

From 2005 through 2010, BNSF and the City of Sioux Falls invested countless hours trying to justify the original concept-phasing plan. They kept hitting wall after wall. The original concept-phasing plan was fading fast, and so was the staying power of the elected and non-elected officials behind it.

In 2010, the rail yard relocation discussion was pretty much given up for dead except for a few diehard business leaders, elected public servants, and city employees. One of them was Public Works Director Mark Cotter. In my first one-on-one meeting with him (Mark would later tell me this was the "first of a thousand meetings we held together"), he provided his "to do" list for the Public Works division. The rail yard project was high on the list.

Mark coached me on the project's progress and the pitfalls encountered over the years. He identified the key players and relayed that some still had fight left in them, including BNSF. BNSF's existing rail yard in downtown Sioux Falls was functional but needed improvements, and $40 million in taxpayer funds would go a long way to make that happen. However, BNSF had the leverage because they owned the property the city coveted.

That first meeting between Mark and I marked the beginning of the most convoluted and difficult project I would undertake as mayor. First of all, the original 2002 concept-phasing plan was not feasible and needed to be abandoned. Alternatives were later devised, but they also ran into bureaucratic and political quicksand. There were so many factors, players, and rules in the mix. For example, federal government rules require public meetings as an integral part of environmental assessments. Whenever alternative for the rail yard project were devised, the public lined up in droves to protest the recommendations.

To make matters worse, time was running out. It was now 2012, seven years after the congressional earmark was approved. About $5 million of the $40 million had already been depleted. We heard rumblings from the South Dakota congressional delegation that if we didn't act fast, the remaining $35 million would be appropriated elsewhere. I had negotiated multi-million-dollar business deals and had already navigated substantial deals in city government, but I was losing patience, and yes, confidence that this project would be completed.

Director Cotter kept encouraging me. "Inch by inch, Mayor, inch by inch," he would always say. Mark was a long-distance runner like me, so we both understood the necessary endurance for strenuous races. Even so, there were plenty of other races involving Sioux Falls city

"Inch by inch, Mayor, inch by inch"

government in which we could compete. In early March 2012, I said: "Mark, let's give this one more attempt with BNSF. Let's get on a plane, meet them on their home turf, and have a real heart-to-heart with them. Either we come together and find a solution, or we are done." He was hesitant at first, but ultimately agreed, and the trip was on.

On March 30, 2012, a group of determined civic leaders handpicked by Mark and I boarded a charter flight bound for St. Paul, Minnesota. It included spokespeople from South Dakota's congressional delegation, the business community, and Sioux Falls city government. We committed to challenge each other and dig deep to find a solution. There was plenty of opportunity for some on the trip to throw in a heavy dose of politics and gamesmanship. At least two of the leaders we invited were powerful members of the political party across the aisle of mine at the time. One of them was an odds-on favorite for the 2018 gubernatorial election, and the rumor on the street was that his opponent in the race would be me. Instead of acting as opponents, we worked as dogged allies so Sioux Falls would succeed in this quagmire of a government project.

The Sioux Falls team arrived at the spacious campus of BNSF in Minneapolis, Minnesota, and was escorted to a large conference room. BNSF representatives joined us soon after. BNSF Railway had been playing a vital role in America for more than 160 years, and the company was a teammate with Sioux Falls for 125 of them. When you are in the trenches with these men and women, you see how they have earned an unending record of success.

After a review of BNSF safety and room evacuation protocols, we got down to business. I kicked off the discussion. I rehashed the importance of the project, acknowledged the difficulties encountered, and that I was confident we would reach our goal. But I did not pull any punches and reiterated it would only happen if we came together as a team. I reminded everyone that time was running out, but BNSF and Sioux Falls could still take advantage of the taxpayer's $40 million investment.

Others from the Sioux Falls contingent and BNSF also spoke, and before you knew it, three very productive hours had passed. After shaking hands and offering good wishes to our BNSF teammates, we drove back to the airport, boarded the plane, and headed home. Sitting across from me on the plane was my supposed gubernatorial opponent. I was thankful and honored that he, along with the others on that trip, took the risk to "fly under the cover of darkness" with me. I will never forget their service and sacrifice.

After the plane trip, progress was still not happening at the necessary pace. Mark sent a letter to BNSF

"Inch by inch, Mayor, inch by inch"

reiterating that if a solution could not be determined soon, the City of Sioux Falls would discontinue its efforts and move on. This was no bluff. BNSF responded, and within a fairly short period of time the company determined a solution. The fix, though not an easy one, was probably in front of us the entire time.

Simply put, rather than building an entirely new rail-yard switching station, BNSF would add two new siding tracks along its existing mainline tracks. The recommended location was already zoned industrial, so that would dramatically lessen the NIMBY battles and public pushback. The recommendation also had low environmental impacts, which was huge. Finally, BNSF agreed to change its operations by utilizing existing BNSF infrastructure in the region at a higher level. It was a win-win for both of us.

BNSF's out-of-the-box thinking put the project back on track. Our work was far from over, with more processes, laws, checks and balances, and meetings (including many more between Mark and me). By September 2013, the necessary environmental assessment was completed. In December 2014, an independent appraisal of the ten acres of BNSF land was checked off the to-do list, too.

Then in July 2015, what was once viewed as unimaginable became real! Ten years after the citizens of the

United States provided the earmarked federal dollars, BNSF and the City of Sioux Falls reached a $27,334,500 purchase agreement for the land. This was well within the $40 million earmark, so about $7 million remained to pay for the removal of the old rail-yard tracks, environmental cleanup, and other site improvements.

On Monday, August 31, 2015, BNSF Executive Vice President Roger Nober and I had the honor to sign the long-awaited rail-yard purchase agreement. It was time to slay this beast and ink the deal envisioned by many fourteen years earlier. The setting was absolutely perfect to recognize the men and women who remained resolute, including South Dakota Senators Tim Johnson and John Thune, United States Representative Stephanie Herseth-Sandlin, BNSF teammates (especially Public Funding Manager Sarod Dhuru), State of South Dakota and City of Sioux Falls employees such as Joshua Peterson, Diane Best, Kendra Siemonsma and Mike Cooper, city councilors, and others that never gave up. It was a beautiful summer day, and I was thrilled that so many joined us to celebrate what I confidently said "would prove to be the biggest accomplishment in the history of Sioux Falls."

With a spit-shined bright orange and black BNSF locomotive serving as the backdrop, I shared a message with pride that ended with this: "Since this dream started way back in 2001, there have been countless men and

"Inch by inch, Mayor, inch by inch"

women who have made a positive impact. All served their country, state, city, and their businesses with distinction. These warriors and heroes deserve our thanks in so many ways. Public Works Director Mark Cotter is certainly one of them. One of my first meetings after being elected mayor in 2010 was with Mark when we discussed this task. It did not take long to realize how challenging this was going to be. After countless meetings with Mark on the topic, he would always end it by saying, "Inch by inch, Mayor, inch by inch." This BNSF 8065 locomotive behind me was built in Erie, Pennsylvania back in February 2014. It weighs 416,000 pounds, with its last assignment transporting cement loads from Pueblo, Colorado to Sioux Falls. It came a long, long way to get here today. As Mark would say, "Inch by inch, Mayor, inch by inch." This rail-yard purchase agreement between BNSF Railway and the City of Sioux Falls has come a long way as well. Inch by inch, mile by mile, on a journey that seemed like a marathon. The tenacious work has been worth it, Sioux Falls. As South African leader Nelson Mandela once said, 'It always seems impossible until it's done.' Today, the rail-yard relocation deal, which many thought impossible, is done!"

13

Play to win versus playing not to lose

When you challenge the status quo, take risks, and serve at an aggressive pace, "stuff happens," and that is a good thing.

It is no secret that you can't hit a home run without swinging the bat, or nail a three-pointer without shooting the basketball. Many people have aspirations to accomplish this and tackle that, but their lack of confidence holds them back. Others never take that chance because of their fear of failure. Government has plenty of elected and non-elected servants who lack confidence, fear failure, or suffer from a combination of both.

I was determined to change that mindset and started with a pep talk to the city council my first week in office. Some of my "rah rah" highlights included:

- I believed we could make government more efficient, productive, accountable, and service-friendly. We could also get a bigger bang for the taxpayer buck.
- I wanted to change the status quo and provided a warning: "Please don't ever tell me, 'we have always done it this way'."
- Sioux Falls could no longer afford to wait on overdue quality-of-life investments.
- We would take risks and certainly make mistakes along the way.
- I would build an administration of motivated change agents.
- The city employees, "our front line," would be actively involved in planning and executing the movement that was sure to come.
- We would set aggressive goals, but needed to prioritize them due to limited time, human resources, and taxpayer dollars.
- We would rally the citizens of Sioux Falls along the way.
- The campaign was over. It was time to follow through with what we said we would do.
- Finally, we would celebrate our success as a community, every step of the journey.

Play to win versus playing not to lose

I believed that Sioux Falls city government had a strong set of city councilors. If they had an idea to improve things, my administration was ready to work with them. I reassured the city council we would balance progress with prudence. I ended my speech with a challenge: "Let's move this city forward at a pace never seen before. Working together, there is absolutely nothing we can't accomplish."

To ensure that happened, I needed to select my own team of department heads and direct reports. This would require a line-up of leaders who would be confident playing offense versus defense. The last thing I wanted were manager types that would fight to maintain the status quo. I was determined to find players that had the stamina to keep up with my fast-break pace. Roster moves within the executive branch of Sioux Falls city government were necessary, and I didn't waste any time executing them. At 8:05 a.m. on my first full day in office, I informed the former mayor's chief of staff that I was following through with a campaign pledge. The position was not part of my game plan. Personnel moves are challenging to say the least, but they must be made.

I made plenty more changes in those early months and when I was finished, six of the twelve departments would have a change in leadership. I chose a team that would embrace change, take risks, make mistakes, communicate with confidence, and bring a proven record of success. I also created two new positions including our city's first project manager and communication specialist. This new administration was rock-solid on paper, and it was time to put points on the scoreboard.

From the tipoff, we took shots, and scored. We accomplished what we said we would do, and more. Neighborhood streets were repaired, airfares became more affordable, aggressive utilization of tax increment financing spurred construction, and jobs sprouted up everywhere. We became known as "America's Next Boomtown!" We conquered unexpected weather events and that dreaded sewage-line collapse. We operated our city "in the black" and added funds to our city's piggybank. Finally, we battled the monster event center issue just like we said we would. Our confidence was growing, and we developed support and enthusiasm to strive for more.

For the next seven years, we went on one heck of a winning streak. It was important to reflect on our accomplishments every now and then. At the end of each year, I asked the twelve departments to determine their top ten accomplishments for the year, ultimately designating 120 victories for the citizens of Sioux Falls. From that list, I created the "TOP 10 WINS FOR SIOUX FALLS," proudly

Play to win versus playing not to lose

sharing them with the media, city council, employees, and citizens. It is important to celebrate that government can "get things done" and to acknowledge the work and sacrifice that makes it happen.

In business, I was encouraged to "throw things up against the wall, and see if it sticks." Tests were often conducted in hopes of improving process, productivity, marketing, service, profitability, and shareholder value. Making mistakes, and some were expensive, was part of the experiment. No matter, we always learned something valuable as a result.

In government, taking risks and making mistakes is strongly discouraged. Government is good at managing, fixing, and sticking with the fundamentals. There is a strong resistance to go outside the box. To be fair, I understand. At least, I understand it now. Mistakes are going to be made, no matter how diligently government works for the people it serves. These mistakes can become the story of the day, an internet sensation, and a salacious headline, too.

There are some, including a growing number of internet trolls, who lie in wait for government to mess up. That is a growing reason why there is preference in government to stay under the radar, rather than taking risks, tackling tough issues, and capturing controversial opportunities.

"Stuff happens" in government, and that is just fine. When you reach higher, take risks, and serve at a more aggressive pace and style, you enhance the chances of a miss every now and then. Delays, lawsuits, frivolous matters, overbearing extremists, accidents, personnel issues, unforeseen expenses, weather emergencies, human errors, politics, and the like will occur no matter how careful you or your team is. Remember:

- "Don't feed the beast," and keep the storylines to one-day if possible. Address the mistake in a timely and professional fashion. Learn from it and move on.
- No matter the facts, some will create their own reality.
- You can't make everyone happy. For those hoping you mess up, disappoint them every opportunity you get.

The famous, "The Man in The Arena" speech by President Theodore Roosevelt conveys a similar message in an incredibly powerful way. It is my favorite.

Play to win versus playing not to lose

The Man in The Arena

It is not the critic who counts; not the man who points out how the strong man stumbles, or where the doer of deeds could have done them better.
The credit belongs to the man who is actually in the arena, whose face is marred by dust and sweat and blood; who strives valiantly; who errs, who comes short again and again, because there is no effort without error and shortcoming; but who does actually strive to do the deeds;
who knows great enthusiasms, the great devotions; who spends himself in a worthy cause;
who at best knows in the end the triumph of high achievement, and who at worst, if he fails, at least fails while daring greatly, so that his place shall never be with those cold and timid souls who neither know victory nor defeat.

If you want to create confidence in those with whom you serve, you must have their backs when something goes bad. As the mayor of Sioux Falls, I was recognized as the face and voice of the city. I was also honored to be a representative of the Sioux Falls city government employees. I enjoyed being their biggest cheerleader, but more importantly, wanted to instill confidence in them too.

The reality for any high-profile leader is that you receive too much credit when things go well, but probably receive too much blame when someone or something messes up. I absorbed a fair share of hits as mayor. When a mistake was made, I wanted to know about it quickly so that we could respond accordingly. When the fire got hot, I did not back away, and fought side by side with my team "in the arena."

President Harry S. Truman, one of my favorite presidents, once said: "Men make history and not the other way around. In periods where there is no leadership, society stands still. Progress occurs when courageous, skillful leaders seize the opportunity to change things for the better." I was honored to work with leaders who definitely changed Sioux Falls for the better, and I can't thank my direct reports, and our city's employees, enough.

I want to acknowledge the courage of the city councilors who were also in the arena, stepping up to secure

Play to win versus playing not to lose

numerous city-government wins. City Councilor Rex Rolfing had more assists than any other, and he rarely missed a shot in his eight years. Other MVPs included eight-year starter City Councilor Michelle Erpenbach, four-year starters City Councilor Kenny Anderson Jr., City Councilor Jim Entenmann, and City Councilor Rick Kiley. I don't want to diminish the sacrifice and determination of the other city councilors with whom I was honored to serve, but these particular public servants were part of an All-Star team when it came to our city's accomplishments from 2010–2018.

The people with whom you serve want to be part of a winning team just as much as you do. It is time to put some points on your city, state, and federal government scoreboard. The sense of accomplishment, and the confidence it breeds, will inspire you, your fellow public servants, and your constituents to compete in the bigger games of public service and life that are sure to come.

14

Don't forget about earned media

Cultivating a symbiotic relationship with the media provides dividends for them, for you, and for the citizens you both serve.

It is no secret that today's news comes to us in dramatically different ways. It evolves more and more each day. The news sources I prefer are the old-fashioned ones. I still watch the 6 p.m. and 10 p.m. news, weather, and sports, and I listen to music and sports talk on the radio. I start my day with a cup of coffee and the daily newspaper (only now I read it via the computer). I am on Facebook, but I am in no way, shape, or form, a social media expert. I have only tiptoed in the social media sea of latest gadgets and techniques.

However, I do feel qualified, and I am motivated, to express the value of utilizing old-fashioned earned media. Earned media is often called free media. It includes publicity gained through news coverage, reviews, word of mouth, and now includes the likes, shares, comments, and feedback of social media outlets.

My earned media experiences started in a downtown Sioux Falls restaurant called the Whisk and Chop. Every Saturday morning during my campaign, I held "Listening and Learning Sessions" to learn about the issues of Sioux Falls and explain my campaign platform. The participants were the "My Man Mike" guy, interested citizens, and the local media. We were all engaged in the back-and-forth banter about life as a Sioux Falls resident. Local television, radio, and the newspaper covered these "Whisk and Chop sessions." They obtained intriguing stories for their slow weekend news cycle, and in return, I was able to get my name and message out there. And it was free!

Earned media proved valuable when I was campaigning but was invaluable after I was elected. The media were always on board as we tackled quality-of-life investments, public-works projects, weather-related emergencies, and numerous other projects and situations over the years. When the storylines and headlines were accurate, and for the most part they were, they played a key role in educating the public and gaining the citizens' support.

Even with the "fake news" barrage that is bantered about right now, watchers, listeners, and readers are still

Don't forget about earned media

energized by good journalism. They are hungry for accurate, fair, and unbiased news. By the way, these same watchers, listeners, and readers are starving for positive stories, uplifting messages, and motivating personalities, too.

The media is an effective partner if they view the relationship as symbiotic, professional, and productive. Communications Specialist Heather Hitterdal, the department heads, and I had a solid relationship with the media outlets in Sioux Falls and South Dakota. We worked to become the most available and open public servants possible.

To a journalist, government is the people's business, so everything should be out in the open or it is a secret. Secrets create a lack of trust. Some in the media and the public will never trust the process if it is viewed as being "behind closed doors." Finding that balance between relaying project, plan, and policy details to the public and the media, while strategizing behind the scenes to execute the project, plan, and policy, is key. In the business world, we worked alone or in small groups, made risk-reward decisions, and then moved on to countless other objectives. It is not "supposed to" work that way in government. For the most part, the media worked very well with me, the city's communication specialist, and the department heads to find an appropriate, even "business like," balance.

The media love scoops. My administration minimized the scoops unless a reporter did his/her own due diligence to earn the exclusive. When my administration called a press conference, all the media outlets were invited. For a fast-break news item, a press release simultaneously went out to all the media outlets. This seemed fair, balanced, and unbiased.

I feel good about my personal and my administration's relationship with the media. I value what they do, and always thanked them publicly for covering Sioux Falls city government. They were always there no matter the conditions, including the weather. The media outlets, especially the reporters, camera crews, producers, anchors, and so many others, certainly contributed to our success, and my success, during the eight years I served with them.

Covering government news must evolve or it will die. It was reported that there were 45 percent fewer news reporters in 2017 than 2008. The numbers are even worse now. The lack of resources to cover important news in your town, state, and nation should be of dramatic concern for you. The traditional news organization is dwindling and is being replaced by a heavy dose of fly-by-night know-it-alls who inject their bias on the news. All they require is a Facebook page, a Twitter account, or a made-up name on a blog to create their take on the

Don't forget about earned media

news. It happened while I was the mayor, and is only getting worse. Can you imagine that two-thirds of Americans get their news via social media right now?

My administration spent countless hours and taxpayer dollars dealing with made-up nonsense from a few that just wanted to criticize, stir up rumor, create falsehoods, or had nothing better to do. The brick-and-mortar news outlets now have fewer staff to actually discover the truth versus the fake or biased news. It is so hard for the news outlets, along with the public servants, to correct the untrue blog post, inappropriate Facebook rant, or salacious Twitter bomb.

Your best defense as a public servant is to play offense and regard the media as valued teammates. Get the details and facts to the media. Work with them to promote the real story, hoping a good share of the citizens you serve will see, hear, or read it. Public servants want to serve the citizens as best they can, and the media, even with their dwindling resources, are trying to do the same.

15

Politicians don't want results, but public servants do

Remain true to the role of the public servant, and fight the urges and ultimate ills of politics, especially partisan politics.

I don't like the word politician, and I definitely don't like it when people call me one. I am committed to be a public servant. There is a striking difference between a politician and a public servant. By my definition, the politician relishes in the games, status, and power far more than he/she enjoys true servanthood. He/she can't wait for the re-election campaign, including the money grab and special favors that come with it.

The polished POLITICIAN often takes the easy way out. Approval ratings are paramount. Being liked is easier than taking tough stands, addressing serious needs, and overcoming obstacles. When faced with a real challenge in government, the politician talks a big game, but then

Mike Huether's *Serve. Lead. Win.*

waits for someone else to take the heat and do the dirty work. Then, if the attempt fails, that politician declares loudly and clearly, "I always knew that was a bad idea." Worse yet, when government succeeds, the typical politician jumps on the bandwagon with an over-embellished campaign narrative about what he/she accomplished, but in reality, had little to do with.

So many in elected office place emphasis on marketing and communication campaigns based on optics versus actual results. Take a look at your own city and state and name the politicians with high approval ratings who have accomplished little by their own efforts. Their "optics" keep them in office, versus doing the work and making the sacrifices citizens expect.

For the PUBLIC SERVANT, serving your fellow citizen is a true calling and blessing. The faith and confidence that people place in the public servant drive him/her to succeed on their behalf. The public servant makes decisions on behalf of all, not just those with power, wealth, and prestige. The public servant embraces the big picture, working for the most good of the city, county, state, and country as a whole. The public servant builds the basics, including infrastructure, public health and safety, quality of life, education, and jobs. The public servant cares about the day-to-day needs of the "Regular Joe or Jane."

Politicians don't want results, but public servants do

I believe most elected leaders start with a genuine desire to serve the public for the right reasons. But some lose focus and get lost on the way. Politicians can rediscover why they wanted to serve in the first place. There is a real joy in serving the public, real value in reaching compromise, real rewards in motivating others, and real accomplishment in being productive in government. These fundamentals keep public servants grounded.

Cindy and I have a goal to visit all fifty states in America, and we have five more to go. We love visiting presidential libraries and reflecting on the incredible adversity these leaders faced. Partisan politics generally fueled the adversity. Political scholars will argue which president or generation of presidents endured the toughest times. However, I believe the current political divide ranks right up there. So many leaders in government today place politics above all else, including their country.

One such example occurred in 2010 when then Senate Minority Leader Mitch McConnell relayed: "The single most important thing we want to achieve is for President Obama to be a one-term President." U.S. Representative John Boehner, a colleague of his in the U.S. House of Representatives who later became the speaker, relayed a similar threat: "We're going to do everything, and I mean everything we can do, to kill it, stop it, slow it down, whatever we can." I don't want to reprimand one party over another or call out one leader over another, because there is plenty of blame to go around. However, it is clear those two statements are not conducive to getting things done in government.

The harsh reality is that this is all about power! The first goal is to attain it, and then, do whatever you can to keep it. The reality right now in towns, counties, and states all across our great nation, is that political parties and their hunger for power control government decision-making more and more.

My dissatisfaction with the partisan divide in the federal government reached a high point immediately after the 2016 national election. The extremes of the left and the extremes of the right created incredible anger and ineffectiveness. Both sides dug in their heels and proved that the congressional leaders in Washington, D.C., and their respective political parties, did not care about the concerns of the citizens back home.

People demanded change. Millions of Americans who were Democrats and Republicans wanted things done differently in government. They registered as Independents. They wanted to vote independently based on the candidates and their positions versus the political parties. They clamored for productive government and wanted their elected leaders to be free to do what is best.

Politicians don't want results, but public servants do

I was also inspired by this movement, and I registered as an Independent on December 19, 2016.

Ever since I can remember, I have been and am recognized as an independent person. I am not afraid to speak what I believe, and I make sure my actions are in sync with my words. I am what I am.

Party labels do not define me. I vote for the best candidate. I support policies and initiatives that are good for the city, state, and country as a whole, even if they are controversial or unpopular. I prefer the middle and have no problem being called a "moderate."

Leaving things better for my grandchildren and others drives me. Making decisions for the benefit of the citizens I serve motivates me. My head, heart, gut, and that deep-down-to-the-bone independent streak with which God blessed me, propels me, too.

We all have differences in our beliefs and our goals, including the strategies to accomplish them. It is good to have passion about what you believe. You should fight for it, too! When differing sides communicate, collaborate, find common ground, and remain professional and respectful, good government is possible. And that is what citizens are begging for.

Statistics show that people want government leaders to work together, find solutions, and be more productive.

They want government leaders to represent their country first and foremost, versus their political party. Americans have a very negative view of our federal government, with only one in four of them ranking it positively. The perception is better in city, county, and state government sectors, but dissatisfaction levels are growing there, too.

I know this is a pipe dream, but I would make all elected positions non-partisan. The mayor's office in Sioux Falls is non-partisan, so candidates do not run as a Republican, Democrat, or Independent. For the most part, party politics have been irrelevant in Sioux Falls city government, and that is one factor why our city has maintained a strong record of success. However, Sioux Falls is not immune, and partisan politics creep in every now and then.

In my two terms as mayor, there were frustrating situations in which partisan politics played a role. This became more prevalent after I was elected to a second term, and the rumor mill about "Huether running for governor" intensified. Some on the city council were pressured politically to take a stand against me, and they did. This was often bantered about in city hall, coffee groups, and among political pundits across the state.

There are absolutely times when we must agree to disagree in government. This should not always be

Politicians don't want results, but public servants do

blamed on the scourge of partisan politics. Remember City Councilor Kermit Staggers? He was a staunch party advocate, and yes, he did infuse a bit of partisan politics at the end of our runoff election back in 2010. And, without a doubt he voted against my administration and me more than anyone over the years. But after serving with Councilor Staggers, I grew to appreciate him. I believe he voted based on his view of the world.

At a media event one afternoon, I played a word game for an online show called Stu's Views. I was asked to provide a quick response to a series of words or phrases. Stu Whitney, the host of the show, relayed the following words: Kermit Staggers. I replied: "He believes, what he believes." And that is the way it should be.

Many of you will serve on a local level versus a higher-profile national office. My advice remains the same regardless of the level of the public service role: Keep the party politics out! The more we play this game, the more dysfunctional government becomes and the less we accomplish. You don't need to be a Republican, Democrat, or Independent to fix a pothole. The same applies to building a new event center, addressing pension reform, tackling an ice storm, creating a boomtown economy, developing a vibrant downtown, and keeping citizens safe.

Mike Huether's *Serve. Lead. Win.*

We did this, and so much more in Sioux Falls. The city councilors and I had the extreme honor to serve. The Republican, Democrat, or Independent registration that each of us had at the Minnehaha County Clerk of Courts Office in Sioux Falls was not our driving force as public servants. It shouldn't be yours, either.

Conclusion

Make the most of the days God gives you, leaving family, friends, teammates, co-workers, and constituents better than you found them.

I have tackled difficult goals, and writing this book ranks right up there. While attending a luncheon near the end of my second term, I sat next to a motivational speaker from South Dakota. He wrote an inspiring book about an elderly Walmart greeter he met, and the positive impact this gentleman made during his life.

I told the speaker/writer that I was determined to write a book or two. He provided me a strong dose of tough love, and said, "Mike, I have had at least fifty people tell me they were going to write a book someday. But I think only three of them have actually done it." Trust me, it takes a dogged determination to write a book, but the sacrifice of public service demands dramatically more heart and grit. The sacrifice expended went well beyond just mine.

My family offered so much of themselves. The love and support they provided during our campaign, and even more so after I was elected, was beyond compare. One of the hardest things they endured was the criticism and misinformation. Many times, it was downright foolish and absurd. There was nothing they could do but take it in. My mom would often relay: "Mike, someone at church said . . . and I didn't know what to say. Is that true?" It often bruised me, and I know it hurt Mom too. Even so, Mom, Cindy, Kylie and my extended family couldn't have been prouder of what we accomplished. WE were honored to serve!

One of the most eye-opening realities of running for elected office is that you learn who your true friends are. In the most trying times of life, those friends who walk beside you versus walk away are fewer than you imagined. At the same time, the process can be healthy, as your motivated partners in life rise to the surface. I can't thank my friends, volunteers, and others that have cheered me on over my lifetime, enough. You are a blessing.

I was fortunate that I had adequate financial resources to leave my employer when I pursued my public-service dream. I know that is rare for most. Employers that encourage their employees, and support their ambition to serve, must be commended. If your employer doesn't support stewardship as part of its

Conclusion

mission statement or corporate culture, find a more suitable place to utilize your talents. Remember, the organization will succeed when the city, state, and country they reside in flourishes too.

Public service is not easy, but, oh my goodness, it was a wonderful experience for me. I loved this public service gig! Serving the citizens of Sioux Falls was truly a blessing. And yes, if God is willing, and the people of Sioux Falls and South Dakota grant me the good fortune, I would cherish the opportunity to serve again. The "My Man Mike" truck has 141,631 miles on it and is showing some rust. No matter, it is tuned up, has fresh tires, and is tough enough for the miles of roads and weather to come. In all seriousness, it will be my family, especially Cindy and Kylie, a few close friends, and God's hand, that ultimately provide the key to starting the engine of another campaign.

For now, the "My Man Mike" truck and I get vigorous workouts watering thousands of trees and bushes on land in Jerauld County in South Dakota. I am converting 160 acres of prairie into wildlife habitat and I love the quest. It also provides plenty of time to reflect on my life and its possibilities.

I have 42 items on my life's "Magic List" that I am determined to cross off before God takes me. One thing I realized as mayor was that I could not pursue these bucket list pursuits at the same time I was serving the good people of Sioux Falls. I have other wonderful choices, so if I don't serve in an elected capacity again, I will sprint to the end of life's journey relishing the opportunities each day provides.

My mom remarried in 1980 at the same time I headed off to college. My stepfather, Earl Merwin Reese encouraged everyone to "leave things better than you found them." His life's activities reflected those words. As a long-time physical science teacher, he left his students better. As a hunter and conservationist, he left the land better. As a faith-based steward, he left the community better. And without a doubt, as a husband, father, and as "Grandpa Earl," he left his family better. This man of Norwegian descent influenced my mom and "his kids" of German heritage with his work ethic, kindness, faith, and wonderful sense of calm.

Leave life better than you found it. This is such a critical time for America, and we need strong leadership among our valued public servants. Our country has incredible opportunities to capture and critical issues that must be addressed.

Take the practical, real-world, and proven strategies in this book and get things done!

Government can get things done!

- The difficult times in your life will lay a solid foundation for the challenges, and ultimate rewards, to come.
- Running government more and more like a business should be relished, not feared.
- Don't let anyone talk you out of pursuing your dream of public service, because we need you now more than ever.
- When you campaign the old-fashioned way, you gain a powerful understanding of what the citizens, whom you want to serve, hunger for.
- Secure the minimum votes required, absorb the hits from the critics, execute the plan, and move on to the next big thing.
- Prioritize the critical items on your constituents' "to do" list, and work to cross them off now!
- The citizens elected you to lead, so take the stand that you believe is best and stay strong "in the arena."
- Embrace the differences of your peers, collaborate with them, and find that common ground to make the impossible, possible.

Mike Huether's *Serve. Lead. Win.*

- Public and private partnerships add strength, vitality, and confidence to the "get stuff done" mix.
- Listen and learn from special interests, but do not become beholden to them.
- Overcoming dire situations and extremely difficult projects requires dogged determination among unwavering allies.
- When you challenge the status quo, take risks, and serve at an aggressive pace, "stuff happens," and that is a good thing.
- Cultivating a symbiotic relationship with the media provides dividends for them, for you, and the citizens you both serve.
- Remain true to the role of the public servant, and fight the urges and ultimate ills of politics, especially partisan politics.
- Make the most of the day God gives you, leaving family, friends, teammates, co-workers, and constituents better than you found them.
- Mayor Mike and countless others across America are cheering you on!

About the author

Mike Huether makes the most of each God-given day and motivates others to do the same. Best known as "Mayor Mike" and "My Man Mike," he was sworn in as mayor of Sioux Falls, South Dakota on May 17, 2010. Soundly re-elected in 2014, he proved that government can "GET THINGS DONE." During his tenure, Sioux Falls was recognized as "America's Next Boomtown" along with numerous other accolades. It was 8 years of tackling issues and seizing opportunities like never witnessed before.

Mike's leadership and business skills were honed for 25 years at Citibank in South Dakota, New York, and Texas, along with PREMIER Bankcard in Sioux Falls. He left corporate America as an Executive Vice President to capture his dream of public service held since the sixth grade.

Mike and his bride of 33 years, Cindy, are driven by family and stewardship. They were honored as the United States Tennis Association Family of the Year, and also named "South Dakota's Tennis Hero" by Tennis magazine. Their daughter, Kylie, her husband David,

Mike Huether's *Serve. Lead. Win.*

grandson George and new "baby sister" Margaret live ten minutes away which can't be any better.

Mike has a television show called "On the Road with Mike Huether" that brings into view hidden, inspirational stories about life in towns across South Dakota. In his "spare" time, Mike relishes public speaking, develops wildlife habitat, hunts whitetails and pheasants, competes in road races and creates special memories, especially as "Bapa Mike" with George and Margaret.

For more information about Mike Huether, speaking engagements, and bulk orders of *Serve. Lead. Win.*, please visit www.mikehuether.com.